BARTLETT

The Great Explorer

HAROLD HORWOOD

PHOTOGRAPHS BY BARTLETT

Doubleday Canada Limited
Toronto

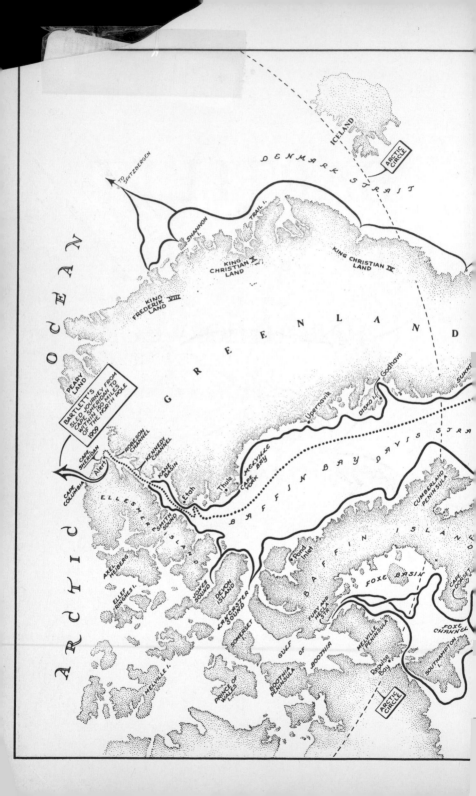

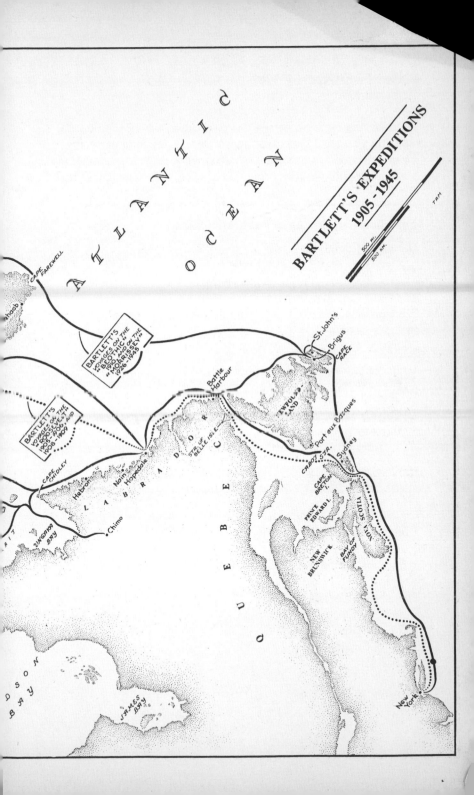

BARTLETT'S EXPEDITIONS 1905-1945

500 MI.
500 KM.

T.R.M.

ATLANTIC OCEAN

CAPE FAREWELL

Shaab

BARTLETT'S VOYAGES ON THE BEOTHIC ON THE "MORRISSEY" 1926-1945

St. John's
Brigus
CAPE RACE

Battle Harbour

BARTLETT'S VOYAGES ON THE ROOSEVELT 1905-1906 AND 1908-1909

CAPE CHIDLEY

Hebron
Nain
Hopedale

NEWFOUNDLAND

STR. OF BELLE ISLE.

Port aux Basques

LABRADOR

Chimo

CABOT STR.

Sydney

CAPE BRETON I.

UNGAVA BAY

NOVA SCOTIA

PRINCE EDWARD I.

QUEBEC

NEW BRUNSWICK

BAY OF FUNDY

HUDSON BAY

JAMES BAY

New York

Canadian Cataloguing in Publication Data

Horwood, Harold. 1923 —
    Bartlett: the great explorer

First published (1977) under title: Bartlett: The Great Canadian Explorer.
Bibliography: p.
Includes index.
0-385-25245-5

1. Bartlett, Robert A. (Robert Abram), 1875-1946.
2. Arctic regions - Discovery and exploration - Canadian.
3. Scientific expeditions - Arctic regions - History.
4. Canada - Exploring expeditions.
5. Explorers - Canada - Biography.
    I. Title. II. Title: Bartlett: The Great Canadian Explorer.

    C635.837867 1989 917.17'2 C89-094142-4

Cover illustration: Vince McIndoe
Design: Ross Mah Design Associates

Printed and bound in Canada by Best Book Manufacturers Inc.

Published in Canada by
Doubleday Canada Limited
105 Bond Street
Toronto, Ontario
M5B 1Y3

TRANS 10 9 8 7 6 5 4

Contents

This book is for my son, Andrew, who already loves stories and will someday want to read about the greatness of his people.

Foreword

This is the story of the greatest Canadian ice captain who ever lived—the greatest, by general consent, of any nationality in this century. Robert Bartlett, who took ships to the north coast of Ellesmere Island and sledged to within 150 miles of the North Pole, made twenty-two voyages into the Canadian Arctic, and six to other parts of the Arctic, but is almost wholly unknown in Canada.

Hardly surprising, perhaps: though Bartlett worked for both the Canadian and the American governments, as well as for privately backed expeditions, he worked mainly out of New York and eventually took out American citizenship as a means of securing financial backing for his voyages. His native province, Newfoundland, did not join the Canadian union until after his death in 1946. Nevertheless, he is now part of Canadian history.

Besides piloting some of the most famous exploring voyages of all time—those of Robert E. Peary and Vilhjalmur Stefansson—Bartlett made four arctic voyages for the American Government and sixteen expeditions of his own which produced, in the period between the world wars, an immense wealth of scientific knowledge. He was the first arctic explorer to place science ahead of exploration.

Bartlett was one of the last of the "heroes," a true Victorian, enigmatic and full of contradictions. I have devoted as much effort to exploring his character as to following his horrendous journeys among the ice floes. Fortunately, he was a prolific writer who, besides publishing three books about his voyages, left thousands of pages of unpublished manuscript, including descriptions of his childhood and youth, not to mention his ships' logs, letters, and other documents.

This book was created from such sources. Bartlett's published writing was heavily edited by a professional ghost writer, who tried to meet certain preconceived literary standards that did Bartlett a disservice. But the original manuscripts survive, at least in part. They are far more vigorous, colorful, and descriptive than the pallid writings of the ghost, and I have quoted from them in every instance where there was a choice.

Bartlett betrays certain inconsistencies. He tended to tell the same stories repeatedly, in newspaper interviews, in magazine articles, in notes for lectures or slide shows (of which he made many). The versions differ in details. Also, in lecturing about voyages of the 1930s he frequently used illustrative incidents from earlier voyages, leaving a confused impression about the dates and locations of certain events. Lastly, he was careless about figures. You can trust his logs, but not his letters or lecture notes, to give you exact information.

So there was a lot of unraveling to be done, and all I can say of such things as dates, temperatures, duration of voyages, and other quantitative data is that I have tried for accuracy, often making great effort for what seemed like a trivial piece of information.

Sometimes I have had to choose, painfully, to disregard something that Bartlett said himself. For example, he was not a lifelong teetotaler, though he often protested that he was. And some of his anecdotes show a taste for embroidery at the expense of historical accuracy. The famous story about his swimming across an open lake of sea water while seal hunting in the ice illustrates this. The story exists in several quite different versions, and I had some trouble picking out the truth. Bartlett was little help here. In one account, for example, he says that when he got back to the ship with the best catch of seals of the day, the captain, as a reward, "offered me a tot of rum," which he refused, having never tasted liquor in his life. The captain on this voyage, as can be demonstrated from other papers, was his father, a strict Methodist who never touched liquor and certainly would not offer it to his sixteen-year-old son in any circumstances. I have therefore been forced to conclude that this is an embroidery, added when Bartlett wrote about the incident half a century after it happened. Wherever I have discovered such inconsistencies, I have simply dropped them from the narrative.

The greatest inconsistency of all is a set of ships' logs, in Bob Bartlett's hand, of sealing voyages on which he never sailed. They are included among a collection of his papers at Bowdoin College, Maine, and I can only suppose that he copied out, for his own reasons, the logs of ships captained by his father and uncles. These documents are real booby traps for the biographer.

I have not tried to hide Bartlett's faults and weaknesses, but neither have I tried to "cut him down to size," to belittle and demean him because he was indeed a great man, with extraordinary courage and tenacity wedded to exceptional gentleness and generosity, as all who knew him attest. He went through life with an heroic self-image doing what he could to live up to it. Many readers today, especially those whose convictions and tastes were formed in the 1950s, refuse to believe in greatness. That is their misfortune.

I had hoped in this book to be able to avoid the controversy over whether Dr. Frederick Cook, or Robert Peary, or either of them, ever reached the North Pole. I began my research with a strong prejudice against Cook, who had been "exposed" as a fake. I ended it convinced that he had been done the gravest injustice in the whole history of exploration and that it was my duty to history and truth to report what I had found. Bartlett I am glad to say, had little to do with the character assassination of Cook, and the charge that he was involved in the disappearance of Cook's papers is not only unproven but unsupported by evidence.

The use of the terms "Inuit" and "Eskimo" presents a conflict, the former being now in general use, the latter being universal at the time of Bartlett and Peary. When I quote them, the people of the north are "Eskimos," when I write of them myself they are "Inuit." But the English language still doesn't know exactly what to do with this new word. "Inuit" is plural. The singular is "Inuk." Nevertheless some writers refer to a single Inuit and a band of Inuits. Also, the word is used as an adjective and by transference as a noun describing the language, all of which is strictly against the rules of the Language of Men. My guess is that "Inuit" will become standard English in all these usages, and that "Inuk" will be used as the singular among purists.

The manuscript of this book was completed while I was writer in residence at the University of Western Ontario. I wish to thank the university for the opportunity to work and do research there. Thanks are also due to the staffs of the National Archives at Ottawa and the Newfoundland Archives at St. John's, especially Archivist F. Burnham Gill; to the library staff at the Arts and Culture Centre, St. John's; to Ernest Chafe, a *Karluk* survivor who provided me with important unpublished material; to the members of the Bartlett family who gave me every co-operation; and to Bobbie Robertson, of the Newfoundland Historical Society.

Harold Horwood
London, Ontario
1977

1

"The finest example of leadership in the maritime history of Canada."

When the *Karluk* went down in 1914, crushed in the arctic ice pack, it was the middle of the winter night. No one on board had seen the sun for more than two months. Noon was marked only by a faint and murky twilight.

Stranded on drifting ice, five hundred miles northwest of Bering Strait, with the desolate coast of Siberia two hundred and fifty miles away, were twenty-two men, one woman, two little children, and a black-and-white cat. There were also twenty-six sled dogs (what were left from the expedition's sixty), but they had been on the ice all along. Ice, on sea or land, was almost their permanent home.

The life or death of them all rested in the hands of one man. Bob

Bartlett, the Newfoundland ice captain who had taken Robert Peary almost to the North Pole, faced at that moment the supreme challenge of his career. He was in charge of the remnants of the great Canadian Arctic Expedition, the largest scientific assault ever made on the frozen north. It was now facing total disaster.

In the early years of the twentieth century, the only parts of the earth still unexplored were the regions around the poles, and a number of nations—notably Scandinavians, British, Americans, and Italians—were busy sending expeditions into those icy wastes. Canada, whose claim to sovereignty over her arctic islands was very tenuous, took no part in this endeavor until 1913, when the explorer Vilhjalmur Stefansson approached Ottawa with a plan to explore the Arctic from the northwest, and the Canadian Arctic Expedition was born.

Stefansson, a Canadian, first sought American backing. A few geographers of the time conjectured that an island of near-continent size must lie between Alaska and the Pole. They backed up this opinion with scanty evidence based on winds and ocean currents. Stefansson was obsessed with the glamour of discovering the world's last major land mass and managed to convince a few American millionaires, but not enough. He went to Ottawa looking for additional money.

Unintentionally, he set off a mild fit of flag waving. Government politicians made speeches urging a Canadian presence in the polar wastes, talking of arctic sovereignty and of "our destiny in the north." A little later it was all forgotten in the excitement of the First World War, but in the early months of 1913 the march of Empire was to be northward. The Canadian Government insisted on being the sole backer of the expedition, but—perhaps typically—the money they voted was too little to equip it properly or to purchase a ship designed and built for ice navigation.

Such ships existed, even in 1913. Newfoundland owned a fleet of steel icebreakers designed for seal hunting, and Bartlett had taken one of them into the high Arctic as early as 1910, but the cost of such a ship was ten times what the government seemed willing to pay. Instead, they chose the *Karluk* because she was cheap, lying unused in Victoria B.C., and almost ready to sail. A wooden barkentine, built far back in the nineteenth century for fishing among the Aleutian Islands, she had been converted to a whaler in 1899. A slump in the price of whale oil had left her idle.

The government also altered the whole thrust of the effort. Stefansson was only interested in discovering new land. Ottawa was mainly interested in exploring what was already discovered, making a study of the flora and fauna, including the natives, and perhaps finding a new copper mine, a hope enlivened by the chunks of native copper occasionally traded by the Inuit of the northwest.

Fifteen scientists were employed and divided into two parties, the larger one to be left on the Canadian arctic coast, the smaller one to probe northward among the arctic islands. Both were to have their main base on Herschel Island, near the mouth of the Mackenzie River, which they were to reach by sailing northward around Alaska into the Beaufort Sea.

Besides the *Karluk*, with ten scientists, thirteen crewmen, seven Inuit, and one passenger, there were two smaller ships, the *Alaska* and the *Mary Sachs*, carrying supplies and five of the scientists. None of the ships ever reached Herschel Island. The *Alaska* and *Mary Sachs*, forced into port by ice, dropped men and supplies in northern Alaska and allowed them to continue by sledge.

Some of the scientists intended for the southern party, to work on shore or in coastal waters, were in fact aboard the *Karluk*. These included the anthropologists Diamond Jenness and Henri Beauchat, who were to study the Inuit of northern Canada, and the magnetician and meteorologist William Laird McKinlay. Stefansson explained their presence on the *Karluk* by saying she was the fastest and safest transport to Herschel Island, the point where everyone was to rendezvous and sort out themselves and their supplies. It seems not to have crossed his mind that she might fail to get there because of ice. Stefansson was no sailor and knew nothing about ice hazards.

The passenger on the *Karluk* was an independent trader named John Hadley. An old arctic hand at fifty-four, he was an American whaler who had settled on the north coast of Alaska and was now hitching a ride to Banks Island off northern Canada, where he intended to open a post for trading in arctic fox, then a very valuable pelt. A racist who habitually referred to the Inuit as "dirty Indians," Hadley nevertheless became a useful member of the expedition when it got into trouble.

There were signs of that almost from the start. Bartlett never liked the *Karluk*. She was not only old but also weak, slow, and underpowered. There was time to strengthen her with crossbeams and to add some extra sheathing, but he agreed to take her north only on condition that she would not have to winter in the ice. She simply wasn't fit to stand it, he said. After they sailed from Victoria, heading through the Inside Passage for Alaska, they discovered that her best speed under power was five knots, instead of the seven to eight they'd been promised. But she could indeed make eight knots occasionally with the help of her sails.

On the first day of August, while still south of Point Barrow at Alaska's northern tip, they ran into a snowstorm—a month early, even for that latitude. Next day they ran into sea ice and spent four days trying to work their way around the cape. When they could see nothing but solid ice to the eastward, Bartlett wanted to turn back while there was still time, but Stefansson insisted on going ahead.

On August 9, the *Karluk* was in loose ice, working eastward near the Canada-Alaska border. She was within two days of reaching harbor at Herschel Island. But the ice closed in and stopped her. Snow started again, and the temperature dropped so low that the sea water froze between the ice pans. By August 12 she was frozen in and by August 13 she was aground.

Stefansson then called a conference of the scientists to discuss leaving the ship before it was too late. They were only a few days' travel by sledge from their first objective at Herschel Island. They decided that a sledge trip would not be practical for the oceanographer or the meteorologist, since their gear was too massive to be hauled by dogs, but the anthropologists (Stefansson, Jenness, and Beauchat) would leave at the first opportunity. Jenness and Beauchat tried to reach shore August 29 but failed because of rough ice and open water.

In fact, the opportunity to go ashore did not come for more than a month. Storms and broken ice intervened. Meanwhile, the *Karluk* had floated off the reef where the ice had taken her and had drifted, frozen into a huge ice pan, first northwest, then east, then southwest until she was near the coast of Alaska again. On September 19, Stefansson announced that he was going ashore with a party to hunt caribou. He left the next day, saying he'd probably be back within ten days.

It was a curious hunting party, including his personal assistant, Burt McConnell; his photographer, George Wilkins; the anthropologist, Diamond Jenness; and two Inuit hunters. It looked more like an exploring expedition than a hunting trip, and that was what it became. Their chances of getting caribou were, in any case, slim since, in Stefansson's own words, the caribou of northern Alaska were at that time almost extinct.

They were barely on shore when an easterly gale blew up, the ice parted, and the *Karluk* began drifting rapidly to the west, with open water between her and land. Stefansson never saw the ship again or showed the least interest in her. After a brief reconnaissance westward along the Alaska shore, on the chance she might have come to rest there, he gave her up, headed for Cape Smythe, and there proceeded to reorganize the expedition on his own lines. After a brief report to Ottawa, predicting that the *Karluk* would likely be sunk by the ice, he turned the scientists loose and headed north by sledge, first going along the coast past the Mackenzie Delta to Banks Island, then northward along the western edge of the Canadian Arctic Archipelago to its northwestern limit at Axel Heiberg Island, returning by a parallel route, long after he had been given up for dead, to claim discovery of the three last islands ever to be added to the map of the world. The five-year sledge journey was the longest ever undertaken up to that time.

Jenness and some of the other scientists reached the Mackenzie and carried out their assignments wholly independent of Stefansson. Bartlett was left in charge of the doomed ship and the remnants of the expedition. His job was made far more difficult than it should have been because Stefansson had taken two of the four Inuit hunters and the fourteen best dogs, leaving him without nearly enough to transport supplies for twenty-five people. At most, the dogs left on the ship would be able to haul four sleds when six to eight sleds would be needed—and not all the dogs could be expected to live through the winter.

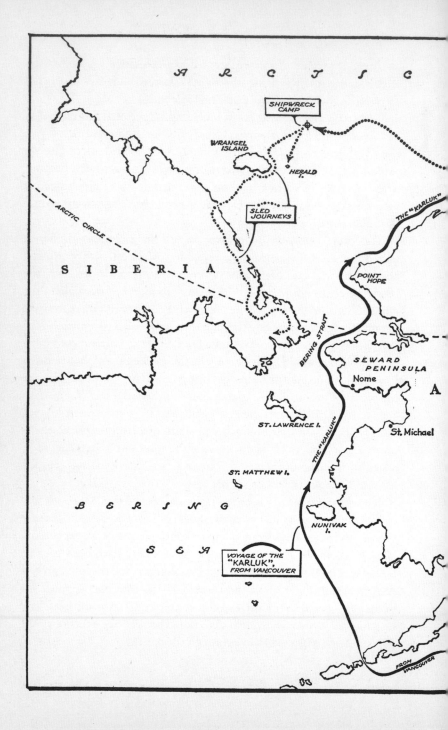

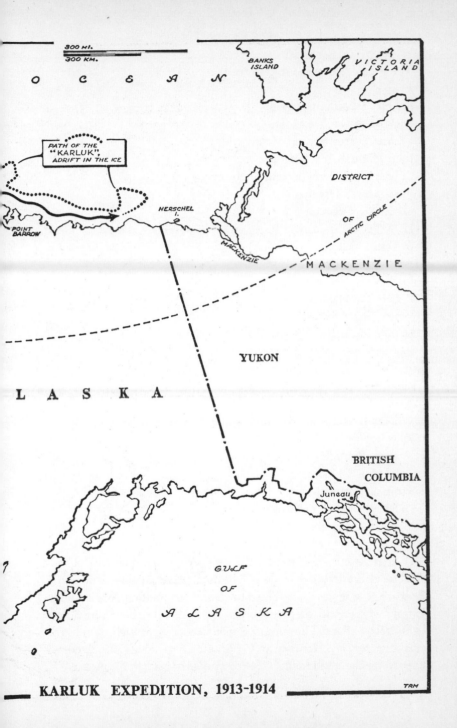

KARLUK EXPEDITION, 1913-1914

The people left on the ship were:

Robert A. Bartlett, Captain
Alex Anderson, First Mate
Charles Barker, Second Mate
John Munro, Chief Engineer
Robert Williamson, Second Engineer
Fred Maurer, Fireman
G. Breddy, Fireman
H. Williams, Seaman
S. Morris, Seaman
A. King, Seaman
John Brady, Seaman
Robert Templeman, Cook
Ernest Chafe, Steward
George Malloch, Geologist
Bjarne Mamen, Topographer
James Murray, Oceanographer
Henri Beauchat, Anthropologist
Alistair Forbes Mackay, Surgeon
William L. McKinlay, Magnetician and Meteorologist
John Hadley, Trader
Kuraluk "Kedrillo," Hunter
Kataktovick, Hunter
Kiruk, Seamstress
Helen, elder child of Kiruk
Mugpi, younger child of Kiruk

Of these twenty-five people, the only two with experience of ice travel were Bartlett and Hadley. The Inuit were Alaskan landsmen whose ice experience was confined to coastal seal hunting. Mackay and Murray had been with Sir Ernest Shackleton, almost to the South Pole, but entirely overland. The only other member of the party who may have been on an ice pan before was young Ernest Chafe, a Newfoundlander, but even he had never made a sealing voyage or been in the Arctic.

The wind and ice drift now began carrying the *Karluk* offshore, as well as westward, at speeds that occasionally reached sixteen knots and that averaged more than twenty miles a day. Bartlett made hasty preparations to abandon the ship in an emergency and long-term preparations to winter her in the ice. The ice sheet in which she was embedded had an area between one and two square miles. Wherever it went, she went with it. Fortunately, it was heavy enough to withstand a lot of pressure and was a pretty safe place to set up a camp.

She drifted westward past Alaska until she was north of Bering Strait and here came within a whisker of instant disaster. Ice driven northward by the Japanese Current met the ice field moving westward in a cataclysm of violence. Crew and passengers lined the deck to watch in awe and horror as the ice fields collided, huge floes pounding one another into pieces, rafting and piling up into pressure ridges that looked like mountain ranges, pans twenty feet thick tilted on edge and forced skyward until they began to collapse from their own weight, and thousands of tons of ice came crashing down in blocks as large as freight cars and with a noise like an artillery barrage.

The pressure ridges forming and collapsing crept nearer and nearer the ship. Everyone was ready to jump, though the chance of living through that roaring white apocalypse seemed slight indeed. If the pan in which the *Karluk* was embedded had been caught, she would have been demolished. But it wasn't caught. The floe, on the edge of the disaster area, cracked but did not crumble. The pressure eased and the westward drift continued.

They now staked out the dogs on lines in a permanent snow shelter on the ice and built two large igloos lined with boxes of supplies. Everything not needed on the ship was moved to these shelters, and a huge fuel dump was established, including twelve tons of coal, thirty-three cases of gasoline, and five barrels of alcohol. Bartlett also ordered the ship to be covered with snow blocks piled edge to edge around the sides and over the decks—good insulation against temperatures that would drop to — 45 C. and perhaps ever lower.

While all this was going on, James Murray kept a number of men busy with sounding equipment and a bottom dredge that brought up samples of plants, animals, and minerals. It was powered by a winch and operated on cables running through a hole in the ice near the ship's stern. So the bottom was continuously plotted and thousands of specimens, many unlike anything they had seen before, were brought up and preserved in alcohol. Malloch, the geologist, was also a navigator, and he plotted the ship's drift continuously, while Bartlett made his own confirming observations from time to time. Unfortunately, most of this work went for nothing since none of Murray's specimens or records survived.

On October 9-10, they drifted across the continental slope and found themselves over the Arctic's abyssal deep, with a mile and a half of water under the keel. The only ships that had ever entered this region before were the *Jeannette* and the *Fram*.

The exploring ship *Jeannette* under Lieutenant Commander De Long had been put into the ice north of Bering Strait, near Herald Island, in 1879, and had drifted slowly northwestward for nineteen months before being caught in rafting ice and crushed a few miles north of what are now known as the New Siberian Islands. The crew hauled supplies over the ice and across pressure ridges in whaleboats to the islands and across the channel to the Siberian mainland, but twenty of them, including the commander, died of starvation and exposure.

The *Fram* was built by the Norwegian arctic explorers Fridtjof Nansen and Otto Sverdrup especially to be frozen in and to drift with the ice. She was round-bottomed and supposedly immune from destruction by ice pressure. She sailed eastward in 1893 through the Northeast Passage to the New Siberian Islands and was moored to an ice floe near the place where the *Jeannette* was wrecked. She then spent three years in the ice, drifting completely across the Arctic Ocean until she was released by the ice between Spitzbergen and Greenland in August 1896. Meanwhile Nansen, with one companion, had left the ship, sledged toward the pole, and then traveled southward to Franz Josef Land, completing the longest journey made over the Arctic Ocean up to that time and getting closer to the pole than any man had been before.

The *Karluk* was no *Fram*. The first time she was squeezed really hard she would sink, Bartlett was sure, and everything he did that winter was a preparation to avoid another *Jeannette* disaster. By the time of perpetual darkness in late November, all supplies were on the ice, sledges had been built, and everyone was busy sewing fur clothing. The boots were made by Kiruk, the only person who knew how to sew waterproof *kamik* from sealskin and caribou sinew, but the men learned by necessity how to stitch passable coats and trousers and mitts. There was no way one woman could make all the clothing needed by twenty-five people for a full winter of ice travel.

John Hadley, whom Bartlett had placed in charge of dogs and sleds, was familiar with the heavy, iron-fastened sleds in use around Nome. Bartlett insisted that true *komatiks* had to be built, following the pattern he had used on the Peary expeditions. These komatiks (which Bartlett called "Peary sledges") were of the eastern arctic pattern, slight, supple, and very tough, with crosspieces fastened by sealskin thongs, not bolts or nails. They rose a little higher in front and back than those used by Baffin Island and Greenland Inuit. Otherwise they were an exact copy of the komatiks that had served those far-traveling people so well for generations.

Hadley didn't like them at all, but he followed Bartlett's orders and made them the way he was told.

"They look nice in photographs, but they're no good for anything else," he growled.

Time showed how wrong he was in this. Bartlett's komatiks stood up to the kind of abuse that smashed the Nome sleds. They were also lighter and easier to maneuver and could carry a heavier load — in fact, were superior in every respect, as McKinlay later testified.

As darkness became absolute and permanent, Bartlett turned his attention to keeping up the spirits of the company. He played chess. He organized weekly tournaments and a grand knockout competition. Bottles of whiskey and boxes of cigars that Stefansson had intended as gifts for the RCMP at Herschel Island were put up as prizes. The Norwegian Bjarne Mamen taught Bartlett how to ski. They built an artificial slope near the ship and another from the ship's deck to the ice pan. They glazed the slopes with sea water, getting instant results because the temperature hovered around —40* and sometimes dropped lower.

---

*Temperatures in this book are given in the international centigrade scale. They were recorded in Fahrenheit, the scale then popular among English-speaking people. It so happens that —40 is the only point at which the two scales coincide.

To celebrate Christmas, Bartlett organized a sports day, with broad jumps and foot races, and spread a dinner that included polar bear steaks, canned lobster and ox tongue, fancy vegetables and plum pudding. It was one of his many arctic feasts, some of which included champagne.

For personal entertainment he preferred music and reading. McKinlay one day found him in his cabin reading a book about rose gardening, and they sat together for half an hour discussing flowers while the temperature climbed up to —30 C. and a blizzard raged outside.

On January 2, 1914, around 4 A.M., McKinlay was awakened by a strange sound, like the strumming of a banjo. The musical note increased in volume, came nearer, then died away once more. All through that day and into the next the humming and strumming note of the ice pressure was repeated. After twenty-six hours the sound had changed to that of a drumbeat and finally to that of distant gunfire. Destruction was once more on the march.

It continued for a week, getting nearer, and cracks began to open and close in the pan that held the *Karluk* fast. At last, just before 5 A.M., January 10, everyone was awakened by the ship's death throes. A crack up to a foot and a half wide had opened along the floe parallel with the ship's side. The deck was slightly canted, showing that the hull was under pressure. The list increased to 20 degrees, then the pressure eased and the ship sank back to an even keel.

As the day advanced, the wind increased until it was blowing at fifty miles an hour, and by six-thirty the ice was rafting around the ship and had punched a hole ten feet long below the waterline on the portside.

Then the pressure increased, and the *Karluk* was crushed, her pumps and pipes shattered, her timbers splintering upward like the shell of a Christmas nut caught in the crackers. Bartlett stayed on board while the others climbed down her sides to the ice, removed the last of the supplies, and took shelter in the igloos from the raging snowdrift.

The captain made himself comfortable in the saloon. Doing what? Playing records. This salty sea dog and all-time greatest ice captain had a lifelong passion for music and poetry. On board the *Karluk* was one of the mechanical marvels of the age, a wind-up Victrola with a huge bell speaker and a collection of two hundred records ranging from popular songs to classics. None of this could be taken on the komatiks, where every ounce must be devoted to food, fuel, and survival gear. It would have to go down with the ship.

So now he enjoyed his records for the last time, all two hundred of them, while his ship settled lower and lower in the water. As each record was finished, he took it off and tossed it into the pot bellied stove, thus keeping a roaring fire going. Finally, after many hours, he took the record he had saved for last—Chopin's Funeral March—put it on the turntable, set the volume on full, and stepped out on deck. The rail was now level with the ice, and water was washing in through the scuppers. As a last act he raised the blue ensign of the Canadian Navy to the masthead (for a ship, like a man, should take defeat in style) and then stepped over the side, watching as she tilted gently and slid under, while the Funeral March gurgled its last and the flag went down, barely listing, and the ice closed.

Then he walked to his private igloo on the ice pan and turned in for a twelve-hour sleep.

When twilight returned, briefly, the next day, the lead where the ship had sunk was frozen over with solid black ice that you could dance on. Except for the people and supplies of Shipwreck Camp, as Bartlett named it, there was no sign that the *Karluk* had ever been there.

In his igloo on the drift ice Bartlett was completely at home. Life had always been a game of chance and one that he played with great gusto. The fact that the Siberian coast was two or three weeks' journey to the south didn't bother him unduly. He had been much farther from land, with scantier supplies. Mainly he was concerned about the members of the expedition who had never had any experience with ice travel. The people he'd have to rely on, aside from the three Inuit, were mainly John Hadley and the twenty-two-year-old Newfoundlander, Ernest Chafe. But most of all, Bartlett would rely on himself.

He had no intention of trying to reach land in the middle of the arctic winter. That must be left for the critical period between the return of the sun and the breakup of the ice. There were lots of supplies, so he saw to it that the igloos were as comfortable as possible, sent out hunting parties to replenish the meat supply, and waited for the annual dawn. Meanwhile he began establishing caches of food and fuel along the route toward Siberia.

The first party set out on January 20 with orders to try to reach a rock named Herald Island, estimated to lie about fifty miles to the south of Shipwreck Camp. Bartlett knew almost nothing about Herald Island but hoped that there might be driftwood and game on it and that it might serve as an intermediate base on the way to Wrangel Island, the next steppingstone toward Siberia. First Mate Anderson was in charge of the party, with Second Mate Barker, two seamen, Brady and King, with orders to go ashore if possible, collect driftwood, and establish a food cache on Herald Island. The Norwegian Bjarne Mamen and the Inuit Kuraluk and Kataktovick were sent as a support party with orders to return to Shipwreck Camp.

Twenty-year-old "Sandy" Anderson was perhaps a bad choice to head even this small expedition. However, Bartlett was following normal procedure in giving the first and most dangerous assignment to his chief officer. He had promoted Anderson to first mate at the beginning of the voyage, after firing the man hired by Stefansson, and he was confident that, whatever Anderson might lack in experience, he would carry out his orders.

Sending the mate's party to Herald Island was Bartlett's only major mistake. His scanty knowledge of the island came from the *American Pilot*. It failed to warn him that Herald Island was almost unapproachable, ringed by cliffs, surrounded by constantly running ice, and totally barren of all life.

Ernest Chafe and H. Williams went out next day to mark the trail of the pioneer parties with flags, one every two or three miles, atop ice hummocks. This took five or six days. Then they were sent along the trail again with a load of supplies on a komatik to be cached about halfway to Herald Island. They met Mamen and the Inuit returning. The mate's party, they were told, had been stopped by open water and had camped on the ice, about three miles from Herald Island, with all the supplies on one komatik waiting for a chance to get ashore.

Shortly after this, several members of the group decided to start for land on their own. Surgeon Alistair Mackay, anthropologist Henri Beauchat, and oceanographer James Murray disagreed with Bartlett's decision to remain at Shipwreck Camp until supply bases had been established and the light had returned, and asked him for enough supplies to start out by themselves for land. A sailor, Sandy Morris, volunteered to go with them.

There can be little doubt that Bartlett's personal appearance had a lot to do with the decision by the doctor and two scientists to abandon his leadership and head off on their own. To put it bluntly, Bartlett who had a plain horselike face, looked like an ordinary jack tar, dressed in baggy pants and a sloppy old sweater. It was difficult for these sophisticated Europeans, two of whom had followed Shackleton (Ernest) halfway across the Antarctic, to think of Bartlett as a leader. A leader should wear a uniform and a mustache, carry a swagger stick, and snap out his orders in smart military style. The fact that this plain-looking fisherman from a Newfoundland outport had led a sledge party almost to the North Pole and back didn't seem to impress them. Their failure to judge Bartlett's character cost them their lives.

After a long and bitter argument he gave way and issued the supplies, but only on condition that they sign a document absolving him from responsibility. He also made it clear that they were welcome to return to the main party if their attempt failed.

They left and disappeared, but not before one of the sledge parties running supplies toward land reported them.

These supply parties left almost every day. The one that started on February 5 was in charge of Ernest Chafe, with the two Inuit, and its orders were also to land supplies on Herald Island. As Chafe described it, they failed to get ashore because of running ice, were trapped in open water on a drifting pan, and spent a night in an improvised igloo while the pan broke up and finally split in two right under the floor of their camp. By good luck they got back to solid ice with their komatik, but without their supplies, which went to the bottom.

Bartlett went out to meet them as they approached Shipwreck Camp. They told of their narrow escape and their belief that the Mate's party must have been lost through the ice. They could see no way to land on

Herald Island.

They told him, further, that they had met the doctor's party, ten days out from the ship, struggling along near the last stages of exhaustion. Despite efforts to persuade them to return to camp, they had refused. They were certain that all four men in this party would perish and that the worst-off could not last another day.

Bartlett was appalled by the news. He was silent for a few minutes, turning it over in his mind, then made a decision:

"Not a word about any of this to the crew," he said. "I don't want them discouraged. So keep your news to yourselves."

They obeyed these orders so well that McKinlay, writing about the disaster sixty years later, still did not know that they had been close to Herald Island or what had become of the doctor's party.

The food caches were set up successfully, without loss of life, but not without grave risks and hardships. Once when the temperature was — 38, Williams fell through a recently frozen lead, lightly covered with fresh snow, and went chest-deep into the water. To keep from freezing to death, he had to run as fast as he could four miles to Shipwreck Camp, Chafe following with the dogs.

Mamen, one of the ablest men on the expedition, injured a knee so badly in rough ice that he was unable to walk at all for weeks and never recovered completely. Kuraluk, on the first trip to Herald Island, wrenched his back and was confined to camp almost until they were ready to leave for the main march. The injuries were caused by the extreme conditions: none of them, not even Bartlett, had seen such rough ice before.

Nevertheless, in six weeks of continuous effort they managed to establish a chain of well-supplied camps, each with an igloo containing both food and fuel. The route toward land was prepared.

They left Shipwreck Camp on February 19, two advance parties of four men and four dogs with two heavily laden komatiks, the main party of nine people following five days later with ten able dogs and three that were unfit for work. Lack of dogs was Bartlett's most severe handicap. Besides the fourteen taken by Stefansson, he had lost others by fighting and drowning until he had only eighteen out of the original sixty capable of working in harness. A lot of the hauling had to be done by the men. Even eleven-year-old Helen hitched herself to a sled and did her share.

The main party had three komatiks, one handled by Kuraluk, one by Kataktovick, and one by Bartlett. They had to leave about two tons of food and most of their fuel behind. On February 28, they caught up with the advance parties, which had actually turned back for camp, defeated by a miniature mountain range of ice ridges, newly formed since the trail had been established. It stretched east and west to the horizon and formed a perpendicular front fifty to seventy feet high.

Bartlett swore at them, called them cowards and fools, and drove them back to the ice wall. Chafe, who had been trying to cross it for three days, says that everybody would have died right there had it not been for Bartlett's courage, determination, and leadership. Convinced that searching for a route would be futile, he set out to hack his way through with axes and ice picks, chopping down the walls of ice until the rubble so produced filled in the troughs and made a trail up which it was possible to haul a komatik, repeating this process over and over all day long endlessly.

While he was building a road across this seemingly impassable barrier at the rate of a few hundred yards a day, Bartlett sent three of the men with fourteen dogs and empty komatiks back to Shipwreck Camp for full loads of supplies.

It took four days to complete chopping the trail through the ice rafters and another day to get the loaded komatiks across. Even after passing the great barrier, they still had such rough ice that they were often forced to cut a trail. They managed to make only seven miles' progress on March 7 and ten miles on March 8. It then took them another three days to bring up their supplies and two more to cover the next seven miles. In a lifetime spent on arctic ice fields, Bartlett had never encountered such terrible traveling.

Because the travel was so difficult, they headed straight for Wrangel Island, having abandoned the idea of Herald Island as a staging point, and never came within sight of the smaller island at all.

At 1 P.M. March 12, they reached an ice-covered sandspit stretching northward from Wrangel Island, a hilly, uninhabited wilderness some hundred miles long by fifty wide, lying four hundred fifty miles northwest of Alaska and one hundred miles from the coast of Siberia.

Many of the party had never expected to reach land. They were so glad to arrive, even at this desolate spot, that they hugged one another and danced on the snow and shouted.

"We were almost wild with delight," Chafe recalled. "No more open leads, no more midnight alarms! In their gladness, the men dug through the snow so that they might touch the earth with their hands, or pick up a pebble from the frozen ground. There was no sign of vegetation ...except for the mountains that reared their lofty summits inland...there was little change in the eternal whiteness."

Wrangel Island's rocky peaks rise to twenty-five hundred feet. The island supports very meager fauna. At that time it was inhabited mainly by polar bears, using it as a base to prey on offshore seals. There was, however, plenty of driftwood for fuel and for building, and as the spring advanced there would be ducks and other birds to help extend the meat supply.

At most it was a temporary refuge. The island was rarely visited, and unless someone could reach Siberia to report the wreck of the *Karluk* and ask for help, they would simply remain there until their supplies ran out and they slowly starved to death.

From their position on the north shore of the island it would be a two hundred-mile journey, mainly over sea ice, to Siberia. Bartlett decided to undertake this journey himself, at once, before the ice became too loose to cross. The first hundred miles would be around the shore of the island to its southern edge, the second hundred across the drift ice. Since spring was imminent, it would be far more dangerous than anything they had attempted so far, so he decided to go with just one other man, the unmarried Inuit hunter, Kataktovick.

They left on March 18 in a snowstorm with seven dogs—too few for safety, but the others would be needed for hunting if the survivors on the island were to be marooned there for some months, as he expected. Bartlett and Kataktovick had enough food for themselves for forty-eight days, and enough food for their dogs for thirty. They traveled around the eastern end of Wrangel, and everywhere they went the offshore ice appeared to be impassable. They were almost halfway to the western end, about forty miles out of their way, before they struck a route that looked passable. Even here it was so rough that it took them a full day to cover the first five miles toward the invisible Siberian coast, somewhere far off to the south.

Then they got into running ice, where they could move faster but with far greater danger. At any moment they might break through a recently frozen lead or find themselves stranded on a drifting pan. Some leads could be bridged with a komatik. Others could be crossed only by using a small ice pan as a raft. Half the time they had to travel far off course, and the second day out they covered only four miles between dawn and dusk. Next day they made five miles. Occasionally they shot a seal, and one day they got a bear, stretching their own food supply and giving the dogs all they could eat. They traveled fourteen days through this trackless mass of moving ice before they got within sight of the coast of Siberia; then it took another three days to reach it. Altogether, the journey from Shipwreck Camp had taken forty-five days, through what may have been the worst traveling conditions ever encountered by an arctic explorer.

On approaching the coast, Bartlett discovered that Kataktovick fully expected to be killed by the savages who, according to Alaskan folklore, inhabited that region and murdered anyone who landed. In fact, the Siberians are Inuit, closely related to the Inuit of Alaska and Canada, though they speak a language that is only slightly related and cannot be understood by North American Inuit. The people of Bering Strait occasionally crossed back and forth in boats and carried on a little trade, but this part of Siberia was four hundred miles from the Strait, totally foreign and known only by legend.

When they struggled ashore, their reception was almost overwhelming. The Chukches, as they were called, took them into their houses, fed them, mended their clothes, and did everything they could to help them on their journey. But of their language, neither Bartlett nor Kataktovick could understand a word.

These people kept far fewer dogs than the Alaskans, and Bartlett had trouble getting even one additional animal for the four-hundred-mile sledge journey that he must now undertake to reach Bering Strait, where he might hope to find a cable station from which to send word of the disaster.

The survivors on Wrangel Island, meanwhile, were trying to reach Herald Island on the chance that the Mate's party might have landed there and were also trying to bring up more supplies to increase the odds for their own survival.

Herald Island, due south of Shipwreck Camp, was about sixty miles east of Icy Spit, the point on Wrangel Island where the main party had established their camp. Chief Engineer John Munro, the only ship's officer on Wrangel Island, was at least nominal leader, and Bartlett had left orders that he was to go to Herald Island with a komatik for the relief of the Mate's party. McKinlay volunteered to go with him. But their departure was delayed by storms and they did not get away until March 23, with one komatik, five dogs and supplies for eight days.

They ran into rough ice and blizzards and never got close to Herald Island. McKinlay is vague about how far they actually went, but if you add up his distances and directions, and add a few miles for traveling at the times he said travel was almost impossible, you must conclude that they were at best no more than halfway to the island when they turned back. Just before their return they had clear weather and a good view of the island with field glasses from the top of an ice ridge. They saw nothing that looked like a camp (hardly surprising if they were thirty miles away) and concluded like Chafe, that the Mate's party had been lost in the running ice.

On April 1, Chafe, Williams, and Munro started with two dog teams for Shipwreck Camp, where there were still large supplies of food and fuel. The ice had drifted so much that the trail was destroyed. They were slowed by blizzards and by snow blindness. But they continued for seven days until stopped by open water. When they turned back, admitting defeat, they were stopped by open water again. In trying to cross a lead on a small ice pan, all three of them went into the water. They got out— fortunately on the right side of the lead—made a camp, and dried themselves as best they could. But the ice was breaking up, and they were soon adrift again, this time on separate pans, so that they lost one another.

Chafe turned his sledge over, banked it with snow, and spent the night under it, not daring to sleep for fear he'd freeze to death. Next day he went searching for the others, failed to find them, and set out alone in the direction of Wrangel Island. He spent the rest of the day cutting his way through rough ice, then crawled into an improvised igloo, unable to make any kind of fire because his oil supply was now exhausted. One foot was frozen. His gloves were in tatters from using the ice pick. It would take him four or five days, at least, to get back to the island.

Then he came to the great ice barrier, spent a full day trying and failing to get across, and in the end returned to the same igloo in which he had slept the night before.

Next day he traveled east (at right angles to his route) until he found the old trail that Bartlett had cut across the ridge more than a month before, struggled over it, and staggered into Bartlett's old igloo at ten o'clock that night.

Next morning a blizzard was blowing, but since Chafe's right hand, as well as one foot, was now frozen, he decided that he had to get to the island or die there on the ice. He chained one dog to his wrist, turned the other dogs loose, and trusted the chained dog to lead him in the right direction.

Through blinding snowdrifts, over pressure ridges, and around leads, the dog stayed on the invisible trail for more than thirty miles. Darkness fell, and the dog continued to lead him, stumbling, through the snow. He gave up all hope of reaching the island that night, but decided that he had no choice but to plod on through the darkness. And then he discovered that they were staggering up an incline. Could it be? Yes! It was the beach! A few minutes later they were right in the middle of the camp.

Munro and Williams had reached the island in one continuous march of forty-nine hours. Then Munro and Kuraluk had spent two days searching for Chafe with a sledge before giving him up for dead.

Chafe had six operations (by pocketknife) on his frozen heel before the infection that resulted was brought under control, but recovered without losing fingers or toes. Williams had to have a toe amputated, a job performed by a shipmate with a hacksaw blade. He, too, recovered.

Before leaving, Bartlett had advised the survivors to set up two or three camps, as far apart as possible, to make it easier to find game, and had instructed them to establish a camp at Roger's Harbor, a cove on the shore of the island facing Siberia, where he thought a rescue ship might be most likely to reach them. Following these instructions, Mamen, Malloch, and Templeman went to Roger's Harbor, sixty miles from the main party. Two of them died there.

Mamen, with the badly injured knee, and Malloch, both strong young men, seem to have died of malnutrition complicated by protein poisoning.

All of the survivors, including Bartlett and the Inuit, suffered more or less from a disabling disease that included severe swelling of feet and legs. It happened whenever they'd been living for a long time on the disgusting mixture that the *Karluk* carried in tins labeled "pemmican." It disappeared whenever they could get a continuous supply of fresh meat. There seems little doubt that Stefansson (who became a wild-eyed food faddist in his old age, promoting a pet theory that people ought to live mainly on fat mutton) had provided the expedition with such ill-balanced nutrition that they were disabled, and even killed, by what they ate.

Templeman, the youngest man on the island, was found by a rescue party from the main camp delirious and too weak to walk. They took him back to the north shore on a stretcher.

One other member of the party died that summer. Some things about his death remained mysterious, but apparently he shot himself on June 25 with a revolver used to hunt seals. Accident, suicide, or even possible murder; the bullet in any case entered his right eye and killed him instantly. Breddy was a thief, who had stolen meat, as well as valuable articles such as warm clothing and a compass, from other survivors, so there was a clear motive for murder but apparently none for suicide.

The others spent the summer on the island waiting for rescue and supporting themselves by hunting. Without Kuraluk they would have starved, since even Hadley was a poor hunter compared with the Inuk, who provided nine-tenths of the seal meat. With only a knife and an ax for tools, Kuraluk also built a kayak, and used it to capture a small walrus. The white men shot hundreds of ducks and other sea birds, but by early August they had almost exhausted their ammunition. The lack of guns and ammunition is one of the amazing things about the expedition—just one more problem that should have been foreseen by Stefansson before he left the ship. By mid-August even the barely edible pemmican was all gone, and they were living entirely from hand to mouth.

The ice shelf that summer never parted from the shore of Wrangel Island, and snow remained unmelted in the hills. By September 1, they had abandoned hope of rescue. Bartlett, they surmised, had died in his attempt to reach Siberia, and no one knew of their plight. They began to look for the best place to make a winter camp, though they thought they had little chance of surviving. Starvation seemed inevitable.

By September 6, they had built themselves a stout hut, and snow was falling almost every day. Their prospects were slim indeed, but they determined to do the best they could, right to the end.

Meanwhile Bartlett and Kataktovick, with dogs enough to haul their packs, but too few to permit them to ride on the komatik, even singly, had tramped the four hundred miles to Bering Strait. There they met their first Russian, a trader named Baron Kleist, and, unbeknown to them, he managed to get word of the *Karluk* sinking to the outside world. There, too, they found a ship, the *Herman*, under Captain Pederson, who took them to Alaska, where they landed at St. Michael on May 28. Next day, Bartlett cabled the naval service in Ottawa.

He then spent the whole month of June and half the month of July trying to get a ship, any ship, capable of making the voyage to Wrangel Island. At last he succeeded in getting the Bear, a famous ice ship that had been launched at Dundee in 1874 to prosecute the Newfoundland seal hunt. In 1884, she had reached Cape Sabine, Ellesmere Island, and rescued the remnants of the Adolphus Greely expedition, after three other ships had tried and failed to do it. She had been transferred to the American Bering Sea Patrol in 1886.

This fifty-year-old auxiliary barkentine, still sound and iceworthy, failed in her mission. Navigation north of Bering Strait that summer was almost impossible. They ran into heavy field ice and made several unsuccessful attempts to reach Wrangel Island. On August 24, they got within twenty miles of it in thick weather but were then driven away in a gale. On August 27, their coal running low, they headed back to Alaska for bunker. On September 8, they were back in the ice, making a final attempt to reach the island, when they met the schooner *King and Winge* with the survivors on board. She had picked them up the day before, almost eight months after the *Karluk* went down.

proves opposite

It is popular in our time to discredit heroism, to believe that it has never existed except in fable. Among the *Karluk* survivors, heroism was taken for granted. The men, the one woman, even the eleven-year-old girl, did what had to be done, no matter how desperate the odds. Mamen made the sixteen-day march across the drift ice with a dislocated knee and continued to act as leader of the party until he was close to death from exhaustion and starvation. Chafe, on drift ice for the first time in his life, took charge of dog teams, faced crevasses, open leads, and storm-driven ice pans like a veteran, and set out on a two-hundred-mile journey during the extreme hazards of the spring breakup in the hope of bringing in additional supplies. Williams, having reached safety after a desperate forty-nine-hour struggle through a blizzard, turned around immediately, with one foot still frozen, and set out on a two-day search for Chafe, believed to be lost on the ice.

And Bartlett, despite errors of judgment, covered himself with glory. His refusal to admit defeat saved the lives of fourteen people in the face of great odds. He received the award of the Royal Geographical Society for outstanding heroism. The Canadian Government, which he was serving at the time, with characteristic obtuseness never paid him the slightest honor. But the greatest commendation of all came half a century after the event from the Canadian marine historian Thomas Appleton, who made some amends for his country's neglect when he summed up Bartlett's achievement as "the finest example of leadership in the maritime history of Canada."

2

"According to their orders."

If Bartlett was a hero in the nineteenth-century mold, consciously patterned on Dr. Livingstone, he was a hero with certain flaws and certain persistent failures. One of his failures was an inability to accept blame, even when he was wrong. His achievement in the *Karluk* disaster was remarkable enough in the way I have described it. But for Bartlett it still wasn't good enough because it showed him as less than perfect. His published account of the first attempt to reach land from Shipwreck Camp reads as follows (the italics are mine):

"On January seventeenth I decided that before long I would send a party of four men to the land to look out for game, see whether any driftwood was to be found on *Wrangel Island*, report on ice conditions and blaze a trail over the ice....

"Those assigned for the shoregoing party were First Mate Anderson, Second Mate Barker and Sailors King and Brady. They were to go to the island with three sledges and eighteen dogs, with Mamen and two Eskimo men, as a supporting party, to come back with the dogs and two of the sledges after they had landed the Mate's party on the island."

He also added, in another place, and repeated several times, "I had hoped they had gone to Wrangel Island, according to their orders."

Bartlett knew perfectly well that they had not gone to Wrangel Island because that was not where he had sent them. Moreover, Chafe had reported to him, privately, that the Mate's party had been lost in the running ice in an attempt to establish an intermediate camp on Herald Island.

Chafe's account reads as follows (the italics are mine):

"Captain Bartlett decided to send parties to *Herald Island* with provisions, and on January 20th a party set out consisting of Anderson, First Mate; Barker, Second Mate; Brady and King, both able seamen; Mamen and two Eskimos. The first four mentioned were to remain on the island while Mamen and the Eskimos were to return with the dogs and sleds.

"The next day Williams and I were sent out to mark their trail with flags, placing one about every two or three miles....

"...We met Mamen and the Eskimos returning. They informed us that they struck open water three miles from *Herald Island*, and could not proceed further. They had left the other four men with one sledge and all of the provisions, so that they could proceed to the island as soon as the ice conditions permitted."

Chafe had no ax to grind. He was writing a simple man's account of what happened, years after the event. He was a great admirer of Bartlett. He was not even writing for publication and seems to have been unaware of the serious contradiction between his own story and the one to which his leader signed his name. I conclude that there can have been no question about the truth of Chafe's account. Bartlett may indeed have instructed the Mate's party to make an eventual try for Wrangel Island, but if so, it was only after they had first landed on Herald Island and established a food cache there. His subsequent denial that he had sent them to Herald Island was simply an evasion of responsibility. He was unable to accept the blame for their deaths.

There was no sign of life on Herald Island when Munro and McKinlay got within sight of it on their relief expedition from Wrangel Island six weeks later. In fact, the tiny scrap of a tent that was there must have been invisible among the rocks, and by that time, perhaps, no one was left alive to light a signal fire.

What had really happened was a mystery for the next fifteen years. Then, in the summer of 1929, the *Herman*, the sail ship that had carried Bartlett and Kataktovick from Siberia to Alaska, stopped at Herald Island and found four human skeletons, a shredded tent, and the remains of a broken sledge. Rusty guns, with initials still visible on the stocks, appeared to identify the dead men as Anderson, Barker, Brady, and King. They had made it ashore, in spite of cliffs and running ice, perhaps already wet and freezing when they landed, and they had died there, carrying out their orders.

To understand why a man of Bob Bartlett's stature could not accept even a share of the blame for this tragedy, to understand why he could not be content with saving fourteen people, but must also try to shift the blame for those he unwittingly sent to their deaths to the shoulders of the victims, we must look back into his childhood in the little town of Brigus, Newfoundland, where he was born and grew up in the years when Victoria was Queen Empress of a realm on which the sun never set.

3

"I fell in the water so often I had no other clothes except my sisters'."

Brigus, the east coast outport where the Bartletts were one of the major pioneer families, was not a rude little fishing station but an exact copy of an English West Country village, with some pretensions to wealth and comfort. It had fine old houses with white picket fences, winding lanes for streets, hedges, pastures, and meadows reaching into the neighboring forest. On the hills above it was a vast stretch of heathland, created by repeated forest fires in earlier times, locally called "the barrens," where sheep grazed and berries were plentiful.

Its crowded harbor also looked like that of an English fishing port. When the fleet was home, in winter, there were more than a hundred fishing vessels—most of them forty to fifty tons, but a few considerably larger—moored side by side so that any boy so inclined could walk right across the harbor near Riverhead by hopping from deck to deck.

There were shallops, as well as larger schooners and brigantines, and a few ships big enough to make regular foreign voyages to the markets in Europe, South America, and the West Indies, where fish cargoes were exchanged for rum and molasses and fisheries salt and for strings of figs and bales of textiles. In March many of the ships, big and small, sailed "to the ice" hunting seals and, later in the year, to Labrador for the summer fishery, loading their holds with heavy-salted cod for sale in the Caribbean.

The Bartletts had been shipowners, fishing skippers, and ice naviga tors for generations. They had supplied captains, time and again, for arctic voyages. No family in North America knew the waters of west Greenland and Baffin Bay so well as they. According to Bob, they were descended from Spanish castaways wrecked on the coast of England in the days of the Armada. If so, these ancestors were probably Basque sailors, for Bob's own features were purely Basque in character, with the long face and heavy lower jaw, almost Neanderthal, that so often occurs in that ancient race.

Brigus was settled soon after the Cupids colony of 1610 and by 1675 was producing enough fish to be noticed in the export census. When the French captured and burned the village in 1697, it was home to sixty fishermen and produced six thousand quintals (672,000 pounds) of dried fish annually.

In 1798, William Munden made the first big sealing voyage from Brigus, landing ten thousand pelts, and the following year William Bartlett went all the way to Seal Island, Labrador, in a thirty-ton shallop, returning with a full load of seal fat. By the middle of the century, forty ships with twelve hundred men were sailing annually from Brigus to the seal hunt, Bartletts going as skippers in one or more of them every year.

It was this experience that fitted them for navigation in the Arctic. Long before Bob ever went to sea, he was heir to a tradition of arctic exploration and of skippering relief ships sent to rescue less-able naviga tors from the jaws of the ice.

By the time he was born to William and Mary (Leamon) Bartlett on August 15, 1875, his father and one of his uncles were making annual voyages as captains of sealing ships, and owned the finest fishing rooms on Labrador, at a place called Turnivik. William Bartlett not only took his own vessel and crew to Labrador for the summer fishery, but also chartered the *Kite*, an auxiliary brigantine sealer owned by Bowrings of St. John's, to take another twenty crews north. These were called "stationers," men who fished on Labrador in summer, using trap boats based on land, as distinct from the "floaters," who fished from schooners or other ships and were mobile, able to follow the fish northward along the coast, often all the way to Cape Chidley at the very mouth of the Arctic.

Bob spent his childhood among ropes and twines, nets and boats, forests of masts and booms, in a harbor so filled with ships and wharves that his family had actually blasted a tunnel through a huge outcrop of bedrock to give them increased access to the waterfront.

He was a sickly baby and seemed frail as a small child.

"I was very small—almost a dwarf," he said. "Tons of linseed meal were used on my chest and tonsils. My, how I suffered!"

"But he beat himself out of it as he grew up," his brother Will recalled in his old age. "By the time Bob was ten or twelve he was as hard as nails."

Bob's mother told a story that suggests the boy already, at the age of five, had the makings of the profane roustabout that he later became. Two Brigus ladies named Pearcey kept a private school, and one day they entrusted five-year-old Bob with a leaky kettle to be taken to the tinsmith for repairs.

"Yes indeed, me son," said the tinsmith, a man named Hunt. "I'll have it fer ye tomorra." Next day Bob was back at the shop, only to be put off until the day after. On his third trip he found the kettle still hadn't been touched. "Wasn't able to get at it yet," said the tinsmith, "but tomorra I promise ye fer sure."

The five-year-old looked up with a skeptical expression on his long, plain face.

"Mr. Hunt," he said, "you're a damned liar."

In summer the boys played soccer and cricket and went fishing in the streams and lakes that are so plentiful in that part of Newfoundland.

"There was no need to go very far," Bob recalled. "I could usually catch all the trout I wanted in the brook that ran right through the town."

But winter was equally attractive. As long as anyone could remember, the Bartlett boys had been in love with ice—especially the sea ice that came drifting down from the Arctic each year to blockade the ports of Conception Bay in March and April.

"From the time the ice came, Bob was never dry," his mother said. "He'd be in water up to his knees, sometimes up to his waist, and he often showed up at school soaking wet." But he never came to any harm. As a small child he had learned to "copy" across ice too small to hold his weight, jumping from pan to pan as they began to sink. It was a form of play that would serve him well later.

"How I was whipped and punished for going on loose pans of ice!" he recalled. "I fell in the water so often I had no other clothes except my sisters'. Sometimes we'd go up in a hayloft and strip off and wring the water out. Sometimes if we were far from a house, no matter, we'd take it all off anyway, wring it out, and go on.... Later on, running the ice floes, these experiences helped us a lot."

As a boy Bob was always breaking the rules, and his father, a typical Victorian Methodist, was always reaching for the birch rod. He was whipped not only for serious offenses but for things that would seem to us utterly trivial—like riding a bike on Sunday. At that time bicycles were still a novelty in Brigus, but a friend of Bob's owned one and taught him to ride it in one easy lesson. He got carried away, forgot what day it was, and rode it right through the main street of town, with results that he hated to recall, even sixty years later.

Among the particular friends of his childhood was the Irish shoe-maker Tom Murphy and his wife, a childless couple with a house full of cats and dogs and a door always open to other people's children. "Never a word about the mud and water we'd track into their spotless house," Bob told a friend. "In the spring we'd come in soaking wet, and we'd take off our stockings and hang them to dry in front of the big open fireplace— the chimney corner with its dog irons as we called them, and its copper utensils hung about as bright as a brass door knocker. They always gave us bread and molasses, too—'loaf an' lassey' we used to call it then."

Bob received from Tom Murphy a gift that he treasured all his life— a beautiful powder horn, elegantly carved, holding half a pound of the black gunpowder that was used, back then, in muzzle-loading shotguns. He took it with him on his first sealing voyage. From another neighbor, Jim Kelly, he received a hand-carved cowhide knife sheath that he took with him on every voyage he made and on every expedition into the Arctic.

Those Irish neighbors treated the boy like their own son. They helped him make his first sea chest and showed him how to fashion a superior kind of sealing gaff from rowan wood (dogberry, as it is called in Newfoundland) with a steel head. The gaff, used as a club for killing seals, also had a hook for towing a batch of pelts over the ice and was considered indispensable for getting out of open leads when you fell or slipped into them.

The Murphys and Kellys may have been partly responsible for the host of Roman Catholic friends that Bob Bartlett made then and later, including priests and nuns, some of whom were among his closest personal friends even when he was an old man and a total unbeliever. Close friendships between Methodists and "Papists" were not the general rule in the 1880s, but the Bartletts seem to have had a warm social relationship with their Catholic neighbors, even with those who lived inside the convent.

Bob's friendship with older people sometimes saved him from the consequences of his own folly. An old man named Perrault, who lived in Kaipokok Bay, Labrador, near the Bartlett fishing rooms at Turnivik, and was married to a Montagnais Indian, once made for Bob a real Montagnais hunting bow that was too heavy for the boy to draw—at least in the ordinary fashion. He took it home to Brigus, and one day in the back yard succeeded in drawing it from a sitting position, gripping the shaft with his feet and drawing the string with both hands. Of course he had an arrow fitted, and let it fly. It headed straight for the house, smashed the big dormer window of the sitting room, and buried itself in a gilt-framed mirror over the mantelpiece.

Taking one look at the devastation, Bob bolted for the back gate, escaped down Church Lane, and hid in the woods until hunger drove him out. Then he went to the home of an old lady he knew. She not only fed him on tea and biscuits and jam but put on her bonnet and shawl and went home with him to mediate with his father. Sure enough, William Bartlett was lying in wait with the birch—"my usual medicine," as Bob called it—but the old lady talked to him until he cooled off, persuaded him that accidents should be forgiven, and the boy escaped a licking.

"I was always on good terms with the old people, and they helped save my hide more than once," Bob said. The exception was his grandfather Bartlett, a stern old man who never laughed, called his grandsons "young varmints," and sometimes took a stick to them. With both his grandmothers, though, Bob had an understanding almost amounting to a conspiracy. They always took his side, interceded for him, and held back information that would have gotten him into trouble.

His parents were stern and chilly fundamentalists—"I would never dare come into my father's presence with my cap on," Bob said—toward whom as a child he was never very close, though he later developed a lasting attachment to his mother. But his grandmothers—both of them—were liberal-minded Anglicans, with fine, richly furnished houses "full of gaiety, cards, rum and music."

His Grandmother Leamon, in particular, had a lot to do with shaping his tastes. From her he picked up a lifelong love of books, and even of poetry. From his Grandmother Bartlett he learned to dance, and possibly also to take a sip now and then—not of rum, perhaps, but of something more suited to a child's palate—"Port wine was only twenty cents a bottle!" he recalled. It was real port, too, brought direct from Oporto or by way of Newman's warehouses in England to their branches in Newfoundland.

(In his old age, semiretired in New York, Bob Bartlett was still collecting poetry from the journals and pasting it into his logs. The stuff he collected was always in good taste if a little old-fashioned in style. He also made gifts of port wine to his friends. There is an interesting note among his papers, a letter from Joe Smallwood, then still a poor journalist in St. John's, thanking him for a check with which he had bought a bottle of port, as Bartlett suggested.)

Bob's grandmothers were responsible for his music lessons. Perhaps he learned his first finger exercises on one of the big upright pianos that they kept in their houses and used continually; but later they sent him to the convent in Brigus for formal training under nuns who held degrees in music. Almost incredibly, one of his music teachers is still living in a convent at St. John's. He never became very adept as a performer (blaming it on his thick and heavy fingers, better adapted to a gun and a gaff than a keyboard), but if he never learned to play music very well, he learned to enjoy it with some discrimination and, between voyages, was a regular patron of the New York concert circuit.

So besides being a hard case, as his brother describes him (every real boy was supposed to be a hard case in those days—you were either a Tom Sawyer or a sissy), he picked up something else from his childhood, something that led him to fill his ships with books, to wear his leather-covered copy of the *Rubaiyat* to a tatter that eventually had to be held together with surgeon's sticking plaster, and to play Chopin as his ship went down—a sort of literate romanticism, a self-image that combined derring-do with a gentlemanly level of culture.

Bob was the eldest in his family. Then there were two children who died in an epidemic. After that came a string of nine younger ones, all of whom lived to be adults. He had no brother near his own age, and his companion as a boy was his cousin George Bartlett.

"They were always getting into some kind of mischief together," his brother Will says. "There was a girl who used to milk the cow—we always had a farm, you know, horses, chickens, ducks and geese—and she had what Bob called a chip on her shoulder, always telling tales on them so they'd get a licking, but they hatched a plan to fix *her*."

The plan was little short of murder. They got a pint-size ink bottle (Carter's Ink, sold by the pint, to be poured into school inkwells) and filled it two thirds full of the black gunpowder that was almost as common as dirt around Newfoundland outports in those days. Bob took off his shirt, wrapped some pieces of broken brick in it, and pounded them to dust. Then they used the brick dust to tamp into the bottle a long blasting fuse that they had stolen from a neighbor. They fitted a cork, sealed it with grease, and planted the bomb under the milking stool. They waited for the girl to start milking, and then lit the fuse.

"It seemed to take forever," Bob said later. "We didn't think for a while that it was going to go off at all." Then there was a tremendous explosion, and the barn filled with stinking smoke. The girl was tossed into the manger. The cow was knocked down. Two horses, stabled nearby, broke their halter ropes and escaped. The boys didn't wait to see all this. They fled in panic. But this time they were caught and dragged before the bar of justice.

"Father gave me an awful trimming," Bob recalled. "The least said about it the better. Fortunately, no one was hurt, and I was lucky to get out of that scrape as well as I did."

From about the age of twelve, Bob was intimate with gunpowder. He not only hunted ducks and murres from boats and along the cliffs but hunted crows and ravens all summer long around the farm. These birds were considered a nuisance and for a while had a twenty-five-cent bounty on their heads. When seals came into the bay, he went out on the ice after them. But this happened only rarely. Usually the seal herds passed north and south a good thirty or forty miles from Brigus; but some years, when winds and tides were just right, you could get a few beaters, as young seals are called after they take to the water and change their coats from white to gray. Beaters, at that time, had little value for fat and pelts but were the best seals of all for meat. Bartlett also confessed, half a century afterward, that as a boy on Labrador he had helped exterminate the Eskimo curlew. Not deliberately, of course. Like most hunters of the period, he assumed that game was inexhaustible.

"How I loved a gun!" he said. "And how opposed Mother was to my having it! It's really too bad we had such a hard time with our parents— you couldn't reason with them, and they kept us from learning the things that would be useful. Obviously it would have been in their own interest for me to become a good shot."

He became a good shot in any case, even if he had to buy his own gunpowder from pennies that were supposed to go into the collection plate at Sunday school (which he did). At least once he and some friends also stole "God's money" to buy cigarettes, then a great novelty, new to

Newfoundland. In addition to cigarettes, they smoked clay pipes, which you could buy in the stores for a cent each, got caught and got a licking. But the boy who got into the worst trouble for smoking was the minister's son. Among Methodists, tobacco was regarded as a sin against the Holy Ghost, and the minister's son, having disgraced his parents, himself, and his religion with the filthy drug, was put on the blacklist for months, without a cent of spending money, kept indoors all day on Saturdays and holidays, and never allowed out of the house at all except to go to school and to church.

In spite of these early experiments, Bob failed to develop a taste for tobacco until he was almost a man. Then he began chewing plug tobacco and smoking a pipe and swearing like a trooper all at once. The smoking went on day and night for forty years. "The only time my pipe was out of my mouth was when I slept with it beside my bed," he said. Then one day he tossed it over the side of his ship and never touched tobacco again.

The harsh rules and the repression and the birch rod all seemed to the public eye to have had little effect on the "hard case" that was Bob Bartlett. There was, however, one telltale fact that he confided to his private papers in his old age: all through his childhood, and right up to the age of seventeen, he was a constant bed-wetter, thus betraying deep-seated insecurity that followed him into manhood. If you could see him alone at night, sleeping on the floor at fifteen or sixteen to escape the disgrace of wetting his bed, you'd see a pathetic figure, vastly different from the roistering older brother that little Will looked up to.

Parents aside, Brigus was a great place for a boy to grow up.

"Winter or summer, we always had plenty of sport," Will Bartlett recalls. "There were two fine ponds near home for skating. One of them was tidal, and when the ice was rough we'd break it up with picks and axes and pass it out through the gut into the sea so it would freeze over smooth." Sometimes, too, you could skate on sea ice so tough, thin, and flexible that you'd feel it buckle under your blades, but the harbor rarely froze in this way.

"We had horses and catamarans, of course. The horses were those tough little Newfoundland ponies that everyone raised in the outports, and we had them going all winter long." The catamaran is a heavy, skeletal wood sled, used mostly for hauling firelogs but good, too, for running free down hill with a gang of boys, or for "randying" behind a pony that you whipped up to a gallop over a well-beaten snow trail.

"In summer we went swimming every morning, usually in the sea, though there was lots of fresh water around. It was cold, I suppose, but we didn't seem to mind—I guess it's whatever you're used to. Then, after school closed, we would move in to the farm and spend the summer there if we didn't go north to Labrador. Father went every year, of course, and all the boys went with him at one time or another."

The farm, only a mile or so from salt water, is still in the family a hundred years later, with twenty head of cattle, some hundreds of laying hens, and occasionally ducks and geese as well.

In autumn the boys went berrypicking on the vast upland of the Brigus Barrens, with mothers, grandmothers, and aunts. They would go for a whole day at a time, taking kettles and pots and a meal to be cooked over an open fire. On these trips, Bob learned how to build fires, even when everything was soaking wet, and how to improvise repairs. In the Arctic, half a lifetime later, with one leaking pot and not another thing of any kind that would hold water, he remembered seeing his grandmother, on the berry barrens, repair a pot with paste made out of flour. He chewed a piece of sea biscuit into such a paste, pressed it into the seam of the pot, dried it well over a flame, and discovered that he could use it to boil water on his primus stove.

The closing years of the nineteenth century, when Bartlett reached manhood, were the greatest days of Newfoundland. The old colony had achieved self-government and great prosperity, owned thousands of ships, traded with them to more than twenty foreign countries, and landed more pounds of fish annually than any other place on earth. It was a land where a boy could hardly escape the lure of the sea or be expected to go along with his mother's plans to turn him into a Methodist minister—the ambition that Mary Bartlett entertained for her eldest son, Bob.

4

"As much as killing a rattlesnake."

At the age of fifteen, with all the schooling he could get in Brigus, Bob went to the Methodist College in St. John's. Despite its name, it was not a seminary, but one of the best general high schools in Newfoundland, with a string of doctors, lawyers, and prime ministers to its credit. He didn't take well to studies and, by his own account, "gave it up after two years as a bad job."

This sounded well enough for publication during his lifetime, but he revealed the true reason in the papers that piled up on his desk in New York in his old age: He was still unable to control his bladder at night, and bed-wetting at the Methodist College Boarding Home, where he lived, was a serious offense.

"If it hadn't been for that," he said, "I would probably have gone on to Mount Allison University."

At the same time he wanted to be out on salt water among the people he regarded as real men. He was not only dreaming about the sea but dreaming specifically about the ice fields:

"At St. John's [the two years at the Methodist College] I used to go on the wharves to see the sealing ships getting ready, and later when the city filled up with sealers—around 5,000 men, crews for eighteen steamers fitting out for the seal hunt—I remember that I had all I could do to hold myself from stowing away.

"When I finally went, it was hard to get a pair of sealskin boots to fit me...the boots were made for men, not boys.... I had them soled [with cowhide]. In order to keep them soft, we made a mixture of Stockholm tar and cod oil—it also kept them pretty much waterproof."

Bob was now sixteen, in his last year at school, but his father let him take time out to go with him in the *Panther* to the ice fields. He was in Skipper John Bartlett's watch—not his Uncle John, a captain, but another John Bartlett, not related. Most of the crew were the same men who fished with his father on Labrador in the summer and Bob, of course, knew them well.

"I was seal crazy," he admitted. The first whitecoat they sighted was on a Sunday, when seal-killing, by law, was prohibited. Nevertheless he jumped over the side and tried to kill the little animal with his bare hands.

Later on, Sunday or no, he and a companion got permission from the captain to kill a few seals "just for a meal of flippers." They slaughtered eighteen.

"Killing these little innocent whitecoats appealed to my sympathy as much as killing a rattlesnake. It's a strange thing how men like Skipper John Bartlett did not encourage me. He seemed to think, since I had gone to school, that the killing instinct should have been kept in check."

Bob's first day as a seal hunter was one of the most memorable in his life. Besides poaching eighteen seals, he broke through the ice while jumping from the deck of the ship, and was almost cut in two by colliding ice pans, set moving by the ship's wake.

The next was hardly better: "It was very slippery, and my chisels in the soles of my skin boots were blunt and much worn down." That day he and his companions were killing hood seals with gaffs—a difficult and dangerous business, for the hood, unlike the harp, is a huge seal, well able to defend itself and more than willing to do so. The adult male, known as the "dog hood," does not run from the seal hunter but stays to defend his family. He is more nearly the size of a bull than a dog and almost as well armed: "When he would rise up on the ice and show beneath the black cap a red cowl or bag and his long fangs of teeth, he was an ugly-looking customer. By the end of the day very few gaffs were left."

The Bartlett crew was hunting this dangerous species with gaffs only because they were low on ammunition. Normally, no one went after the hood seal with anything less deadly than a gun. Hand-to-hand combat was foolhardy.

Next day the neophite seal hunter suffered for his heroics: "I was pretty stiff, and my testicles were swollen beyond all belief. I had to get the steward, Billy Horwood, to make a bag and arrange it so that they would not hang down. But as the day wore on, I seemed to get better."

In describing this first sealing voyage of his, Bob Bartlett unwittingly settled the controversy about whether Newfoundland sealers ever skinned seals alive or not. He reported in his unpublished papers, written long before the controversy began, that he often saw seals skinned alive. His description of the butchering of an adult hood seal (for which he had no feeling of compassion, remember) is as follows:

"Two men, as a rule, tackle him, hitting him in the windpipe and under the chin [with steel-tipped wooden gaffs]...it really was hard to tell when they were dead.... One man would plant the point of the steel gaff through his lip, holding it with all his weight on the gaff, then the other man...would make the cut with the knife from the throat to the tail. Then they would work the knife between the carcass and the fat, and not until the carcass was separated from the pelt would the man who had his gaff in his lip let go. Later on I have seen the old dogs, even after the flipper strings were cut, turn over and struggle and work their flippers, sometimes scratching the man who was sculping very badly."

In three days the Bartlett crew had killed a load, and began hauling the pelts and fat on board. Carcasses were left on the ice, to be eaten by gulls, fish, and marine invertebrates. While they were doing this, the ship got jammed between closing ice pans four feet thick and had to jettison most of her coal to lighten herself. The ice then rafted under her keel and lifted her out of the water, breaking rudder and propeller as it did so. Then it parted and she floated again. Sealing ships carried spare rudders and propellers as standard equipment. Working on the ice pans, half immersed in water, the sealers fitted and bolted them in place, and the ship was seaworthy once more.

By now she was loaded deep with fat—loaded beyond her legal safety limit, in fact—and they headed for home. The crew that year shared $63.90—a "good voyage" by the standards of the nineteenth century, when a sealer who made fifty dollars for risking his life among the ice floes was regarded as exceedingly lucky. Bob used his share to pay the first premium on his first insurance policy—a thirty-year endowment. (He collected it when it matured in the 1920s, along with three others. They helped tide him over the lowest ebb of his life.)

Bob was still sixteen when his first sealing voyage ended. He went back to school and passed his final year, without any academic distinction. His mother still hoped to see him go to college and study for the ministry, but his father didn't care in the least whether he followed the sea or a career ashore. At the age of seventeen the boy joined one of his father's fishing crews and even had temporary command of a schooner for a few weeks on the Labrador coast. That autumn, when instead of returning to school Bob decided to sign on as ordinary seaman for a foreign voyage—the first step toward becoming an officer and eventually a master mariner—his father promptly concurred in the plan, and even his mother, after some persuasion, said she wouldn't try to stop him. The story that he ran away to sea, like a lot of other published material about him, is utterly untrue.

Mary Bartlett packed a well-stocked sea bag for her son, filled mostly with woolen clothes that he didn't wear until the last days of the voyage. He sailed in the barkentine *Corisande* with fish for Brazil—one of the prime Newfoundland markets—and two days out of St. John's was working on deck in cotton dungarees and bare feet while the people at home were getting out their long johns and flannel undershirts.

But it wasn't much of a holiday. Except for the long leg of the voyage when they sailed with the trade winds, he had to work twelve hours a day—watch on deck and watch below, as it was called—bracing yards, reefing, tacking, and wearing ship, and attending to the endless rope-work, aloft and alow, that made up the management of a square-rigger, the fastest and most beautiful sailing ship ever created but by no means easy to sail. That, perhaps, was why most governments continued to insist that mates and captains must learn their seamanship in such vessels long after steamships had replaced them for most of the world's trade.

Having discharged fish at Pernambuco, the *Corisande* sailed for the West Indies, took on a cargo of fisheries salt, and headed for home. At the same time Bob Bartlett was promoted from ordinary seaman to able seaman, and was given a berth aft—a place that belonged by right to the second mate. But the second mate of the *Corisande* was an eccentric who preferred to live in the forecastle with the crew rather than in the cabins with the officers. Bob was already an officer-to-be, serving his apprenticeship under sail, so there was no objection to giving such a young sailor the place of honor aft.

Off Cape Cod, on the way north, they ran into cold weather and got back into sea boots and oilskins. From there to Cape Race it was a constant battle against winter storms. After getting in over the edge of the banks, they ran into freezing spray and had to chop ice from the standing rigging in order to keep the ship from becoming top-heavy and in danger of capsizing. It was hard work, performed in miserable conditions, exactly the sort of thing that was supposed to make first-class seamen out of green apprentices.

On the last night of the voyage, as they approached land, they were making around ten knots, with smooth water but a stiff southeast wind and snow.

Bob could hear murres flying about the ship and saw them passing close to the red running light on the portside—the lee side, away from wind and snow.

"We are not far from land, sir," he told the mate, for these duck-sized sea birds stay close to shore, especially in winter.

"[When we went off watch] the mate told me not to take off my clothes, not even my mittens and southwester," he wrote later. "We dropped into our bunks in our oilskins, and left the kerosene lamp burning.

"The watch was relieved at four o'clock in the morning, the Mate turning her over to the bosun. It was as dark as the grave. I had the wheel from two o'clock to four o'clock, and as soon as my head struck the pillow I was fast asleep....

"I dreamt that I was in the mizzen rigging of the *Corisande*. It was blowing a gale, and in my arms I held an infant. Alongside of me was Father F. W. Browne, who at one time was the Monsignor's assistant at Brigus.

"He was trying to baptize the baby, and it was bawling lustily, as he was reaching to get the water from a pitcher he had in his hand. It capsized, and the water came over me. It was cold! And I awakened just as the steward sang out, 'Land—Mr. Webber!'"

Bob hit the deck at a run, discovered the Mate hadn't wakened, and went back for him. They found the captain at the wheel and the ship so close to the cliffs that she'd lost both wind and steerageway. A sailing ship, caught in this position, cannot be worked offshore. If the tide will not take her out, the only thing you can do is try to ground her as safely as possible. After a minute or so trying to make her sail, the Mate reported to the captain, "It's no use, sir. Better put her hard up, and let her go in headfirst."

"The jib sheets were hauled to windward, and the main and mizzen sheets slacked off," Bob recalled. This brought her head around. "The yards were squared about a minute or so before she struck. She could not have gone in a better place. We went in over a breaker. It was at high water.... At first we intended chopping down the foremast to make a bridge so we could get to the land, but the height of the cliffs was too great.

"It must have been around five o'clock when she struck. She impaled her starboard bow on the rocks.... Daylight came very slowly. It was dark almost to eight o'clock. Thick snow again began falling but no wind or frost. We now began, as the dawn came, to hoist out the boats and to swing them clear of the rail.... The rock we went over was now breaking, and the sea was making fast—the wind had veered....

"While waiting for daylight I got my chest open.... I had twenty English sovereigns tied in a handkerchief. Then I took off all my clothes to the naked buff and put on clean clothes.

"When the light came the boats were lowered, and the captain's boat went out first, then the longboat. As we were going out, the rock broke and filled the longboat...fortunately we had three or four oak buckets...so we soon freed the boat of water. I wasn't very wet because I had on my oilskins, tied down at the bottom of the legs, and the same at the ends of the sleeves....

"We followed the shore at the Mate's orders, to the westward. Bye-and-bye we came to a cove, and there were houses. They belonged to the fishermen. No one was living in them now. The fishermen who owned and occupied them in the fishing season lived in the bay and over at Trepassey. This was called Brestia Cove, seven miles from Trepassey Drook, and ten or twelve miles from Trepassey.

"Where we struck was Mistaken Point, five or six miles to the westward of Cape Race...and the gulch which we went into in the *Corisande* was the Devil's Chimney.

"A river ran into the cove, and up it we dragged the boats. Then we entered one of the houses, found stoves and kindling, so we put up the pipes and started a fire....

"I went off to see if I could find where the vessel was. I did get over to where she had stranded, but the sea, which rapidly rose with the veering of the wind, soon finished her. Two hours after we left her there wasn't a thing but...flotsam and jetsam....

"Just at dusk a gang of fishermen came...with ropes and axes as sharp as razors...it was bitterly cold. The wood in the houses cracked under the severe frost, and the reports were like pistol shots...no one slept—the frost was pretty keen outside, but within all was warmth and comfort. Plenty wood, and the stove was red all the time....

"At the first crack of dawn we were on our way to Trepassey Drook.

Here I met several men who in the past had saved many lives, and one man in particular had medals, watches, and telescopes from almost every seafaring nation in the world. He had been lowered over the cliffs many times, bringing up arms, legs, and trunks of bodies washed on shore in the clefts of the rock. I saw the cemetery where they were buried. Finally we reached Trepassey and got word home to Brigus that we were safe."

From Trepassey they went by coastal steamer to Placentia and from there by rail to Brigus. At Whitbourne, on the way, Bob met the very Father Browne whom he had seen in a dream on the night of the shipwreck. His mother had cabled the priest and asked him to meet her son. A good thing she did, too, because while they were talking a policeman boarded the train to arrest Bob for theft and take him to the jail in St. John's. Only the presence of the priest convinced the policeman that, somehow or other, he was arresting the wrong man. As it turned out, another sailor had stolen the conductor's topcoat and uniform and had stored them in Bartlett's sea bag. The matter was finally straightened out and Bob went home while his shipmate went to jail.

That spring he went seal hunting for the second time. In April, out gunning for old seals (the whitecoats were always clubbed to death, the adults, hard to catch and possibly dangerous, were usually shot), he came to an open lead with a fine patch of old harp seals on the other side. Without hesitation he stripped, swam across the water, and struggled out on the ice. His clothes and gun were tossed across by his companions. He then went on to kill the seals and eventually to get back to the ship with the biggest catch of the day.

This story—often told in versions that are quite incredible and untrue—is well authenticated. It becomes more believable when you remember that the Bartlett boys were used to swimming in sea water in May and June when the water temperature was only a few degrees above freezing, and that they'd always made a ritual of swimming in a fresh-water lake on the twenty-fourth of May (Queen Victoria's birthday and a general holiday throughout her empire) even if snow happened to be falling.

On his plunge after the seals, Bob was probably less than a minute in the sea water. Then he dressed in warm clothes and was, in fact, far better off than someone who had fallen in with his clothes on, as sealers often did. The incident impressed his companions, however, most of whom could not swim at all, much less in ice water; and to some extent it even impressed the tough old captain, who is reported to have met him on deck with the scant words of praise, "You'll do, boy, you'll do."

Bob by now had learned enough practical navigation to find a ship's position accurately and knew enough mathematics to continue his studies as a theoretical navigator. But it would be five years before he could qualify as a master with a ticket. Meanwhile, he could become skipper of a fishing ship—and did, at the age of eighteen.

That summer, when they were fitting out for the Labrador fishery, Bob went to his father and asked for the command of their schooner, the *Osprey*. He had skippered her briefly the year before on the Labrador coast, but this would be a very different proposition. He would have to sail far from land on a voyage where be might log two thousand miles or even more and through some of the most dangerous waters in the world. His brother Will says that Bob laid down the law on the matter: either he'd be given command of the ship or he wouldn't go fishing at all.

William Bartlett, at first skeptical, demanded a practical demonstration of his son's skill with sextant and chronometer as well as chart and compass, but Bob satisfied him and got the ship. It was his first important command, and he succeeded in bringing home a good load of fish. Beginner's luck. Bob was no fisherman. He tried it a number of times later, but that first fishing voyage was the only truly successful one in his life.

After that he continued sealing every spring and proved to be an excellent Master Watch, in charge of ice parties, and a good Second Hand, in charge of the ship under a captain. But when he finally rose to the command of sealing ships, his luck proved no better as a sealer than it was as a fisherman.

Meanwhile, except for the few weeks each spring of the annual seal hunt, he continued to "go foreign," as Newfoundlanders called it when you sailed on a trading ship. He spent four years almost continuously in square-riggers, about half the time in the tropics, carrying bananas, coal, salt, and general cargo, mostly north and south to the West Indies and

Latin America but sometimes to Europe and the Mediterranean as well. At the age of twenty-two, he had put in the necessary time at sea; he sat for his examinations and scored his captain's ticket.

Later that same year he met Robert Peary, the American polar fanatic who was determined to be the first man to stand at the very top of the earth.

5

"Next voyage I'm going to the North Pole."

In the spring of 1898, Bob Bartlett was invited by his uncle, John Bartlett, to sail to Ellesmere Island as first mate of the Windward, the flagship of Peary's North Pole Expedition. The supply ship Hope was in charge of another uncle, Sam Bartlett, who had orders to go as far as Etah, the Inuit village at the northwest corner of Greenland, where Kennedy Channel empties into Baffin Bay. The *Windward* was to continue northward through Kane Basin and Robeson Channel to the north coast of Ellesmere Island (Grant Land, as Peary called it) if she could get that far.

Near the northeast corner of Ellesmere was a small station called Fort Conger, established by the Greely expedition a few years earlier.

† This and other errors reported by Peary continued to appear on American maps and charts for the next thirty years or more.

* Peary planned to take over this station with its small wooden shacks and supplies and to make it his most southerly base. Another was to be set up at Cape Sheridan (Cape Rawson on modern maps), sixty miles north of Fort Conger, and a third and final one at Cape Columbia, ninety miles farther to the northwest, the most northerly point in Canada, lying on the seventieth degree of longitude, four hundred and thirty miles from the pole. This was described by Peary as "the American route to the pole" because at that time the Americans did not recognize Canada's sovereignty over Ellesmere Island and because explorers of various European nations were trying to reach the pole by way of Spitzbergen (Svalbard) or northern Greenland.

Peary's plan was simple but ambitious. It was to sledge huge quantities of supplies to this most northerly base using scores of Inuit and hundreds of dogs to do so, then to send out parties to break trail across the sea ice and establish supply depots, a fresh party setting out on the heels of each trail blazer, each party going farther than its predecessor, until its supplies were nearly exhausted, then heading back to land, leaving him a clear trail over which he could sledge all the way to the pole.

This was Peary's first attempt to get into the Arctic Ocean by ship. Previously he had tried sledging over the Greenland ice cap, had discovered Peary Land, the ice-free peninsula on Greenland's north coast, and had reported incorrectly that it was a large separate island, divided from Greenland by the Peary Channel.† Although it was about twenty miles closer to the pole than the north coast of Ellesmere Island, he had ruled out Peary Land as a jumping-off place because of the long and difficult sledge journey over the ice cap.

Bob was commissioned by Captain John Bartlett to hire a crew of Newfoundlanders and to take them to New York to join the *Windward*. They arrived on June 10, dressed for the Arctic, in the middle of a heat wave. The *Windward* was lying at a Tompkinsville (Staten Island) dock.

---

* Lieutenant A.W. Greely, U.S. Army Signal Corps, had been sent north to establish bases on the shore of the Arctic Ocean. Marooned at Fort Conger in 1883, when his supply ship was wrecked, Greely and his men fought their way southward on foot for two hundred miles, starving to death and even eating one another, until only eight of the original twenty-six remained. One of Bob Bartlett's uncles was ice captain on the expedition that eventually rescued the few survivors.

She had been presented as a gift to Peary by Lord Northcliffe, who was a wealthy tycoon as well as an aristocrat, and had taken fifty-six days to sail across the Atlantic—one of the longest ice-free passages in modern times. In addition to her square sails, she had an inadequate little coal-fired engine that was about ready to expire. Water had gotten from the bilges into the machinery. The boiler had a patch that blew out the first time it was fired.

Bob set to work to get this decrepit old ship into seaworthy condition. While he was doing this and taking supplies on board, Peary, in the *Hope*, sailed for Etah. At last all was ready and John Bartlett arrived, hoping to make a race of it with his brother Sam, despite the head start that the *Hope* enjoyed.

They sailed July 3, 1898, and quickly discovered that the *Windward's* twenty-five-horsepower engine was not even able to buck the inflowing tide in the East River. They had to anchor and wait for the tide to turn. An ignominious beginning, but hardly surprising. Those old auxiliary brigantines were not really intended as steamships. The job of their little engines was solely to take them in and out of port, so avoiding towing fees, or to keep them moving in a dead calm. During most of the voyage the *Windward* relied on her sails alone.

First port of call was Sydney, Nova Scotia, where they took on all the coal they could carry, on deck or below. They loaded and left harbor as quickly as possible, three days behind the *Hope*.

John Bartlett seems to have been a foolhardy driver of a captain, even by Bob's standards, which weren't very exacting, for he himself was no paragon of caution when it came to handling a ship.

"Uncle John," he reported, "issued orders to carry every rag we had, and not to shorten sail no matter how hard it blew, or how foggy it became...in my forty years at sea I've never seen a captain drive a ship the way he did...we made ten or eleven knots under sail alone, and sometimes twelve. With a full-bodied ship like the *Windward*, it requires the hardest kind of driving and a willingness to risk the spars, if not the vessel herself, to log such a speed."

There were just three men on deck at each watch—one to handle the wheel and two for the sails. For a square-rigger, it was seriously short-handed, and few sailors other than Newfoundlanders would have accepted work in such conditions. But Peary never had a cent to spare: his ships were always undermanned and his sailors always underpaid.

Near the middle of Davis Strait, between Greenland and Baffin Island, they ran into a gale and a snowstorm.

"When I came up for my watch at 4 A.M., it was so thick you couldn't see the bow from the stern," Bob recalled. "With the wind two points abaft the beam and blowing great guns, she was booming along with every spar and timber groaning, the lee rail under. I asked Uncle John for permission to shorten sail, for not only were we in imminent danger of being dismasted, but we were in an area abounding with icebergs. Without even looking up from the Bible he was reading, he harked at me, 'When the proper time comes for taking in sail I'll issue the necessary orders.'... Feeling like a man who has just heard his death sentence pronounced, I took my place on the bridge.

"Several hours passed, and everything held; innumerable bergs slithered past, but in the blinding snow they seemed more like gray shadows than granite-hard islands of ice. My terror was beginning to subside when suddenly the robands parted from the head of the main topgallant sail with a bang, like the report of a three-inch gun. There was no time to think, for the sail was thrashing to pieces. Almost before we knew it, Jimmie Golf and I were out on the yardarm trying to secure the remnants, leaving Tom Hickey at the wheel to carry on as best he could."

One of the faults in the design of those old ships was the location of the wheel—hidden behind the bridge, with a deckhouse in front, so that the wheelsman could see nothing ahead and had to be directed as to every move by a man on lookout duty. Tom did his best by trying to peer past the wing of the bridge, but he could see very little.

Bob and the other sailor were both far above the deck, making fast what remained of the highest sail on the ship, when they happened to glance up and see, almost dead ahead, but a trifle on the lee bow, a towering pyramid of ice toward which the ship was charging at a speed of eleven or twelve knots. If she struck it, she'd smash herself to matchwood.

"We both let out a wild yell, but in that howling gale we would have

been lucky to make ourselves heard with a siren. Tom was trying to get
a squint forward past the wing of the bridge. Just as we braced ourselves
for the crash, he lost his balance for an instant . . . he had leaned a little
too far outboard. A big wave struck the quarter at the crucial moment
and kicked the wheel out of his hands. The ship took charge. She
broached wildly. We shot past the berg, and in a twinkling it was
swallowed up astern. Meanwhile, oblivious to what was almost hanging
over the lee rail, Tom was struggling to get the vessel back on her course,
with one eye still cocked ahead. When the shaking sailormen finally
regained the deck and staggered aft to the bridge, wiping icy sweat from
their brows, Tom greeted us with loud guffaws and asked if we had seen
the *Flying Dutchman* or what."

After two days of such hair-raising risks, they got the *Windward* across
Davis Strait and ran into the ice from the East Greenland Current. This
ice stream is swept down the east coast of Greenland by water flowing
along the surface out of the Arctic Ocean, around Cape Farewell at
Greenland's southern tip, and then northward as far as Godthaab, the
site of an ancient Norse settlement almost three hundred miles northwest of the cape. In the summer of 1898 the ice was unusually heavy, and
they could not approach the Greenland coast until they got north of
Sukkertoppen, opposite Baffin Island's Cumberland Peninsula.

Then they had clear sailing in Baffin Bay—the "North Water" of the
whalers, where the ocean is always in part ice-free—past the spectacular
mountains of Disko Island and the towering ice front of Melville Bay
where the mile-thick glaciers calve into huge bergs that float free and
drift gradually southward to plague shipping for more than two thousand
miles before they are finally melted in mid-Atlantic by warm water from
the Gulf Stream.

At the Inuit village of Etah they rendezvoused with the Hope, which
had beaten them by a day, took all her supplies, and filled their deck with
dogs, komatiks, and people collected from various parts of Davis Strait
by Peary. At this point he boarded the *Windward* and sent the *Hope* back
to Newfoundland. The exact number of Inuit who took part in this
expedition is not on record, so far as I know. Bartlett described them as
"about a dozen families ,"which would mean fifty or sixty people.

Despite his long association with the "Polar Eskimos," as he chose to call the people of northwest Greenland, Robert Peary had never learned to speak their language and had no interpreter. He got by with a few single words, many gestures, and a lot of drawing. Before he was finished with his expeditions, some of the Inuit were beginning to speak a little English, but in 1898 the language barrier was still almost complete.

Peary had an Inuit common-law wife—Allakasingwah—in addition to his American wife at home, and he fathered several children in Greenland, though he never acknowledged them, provided for them, learned to speak their language, or taught them his. His friends never mentioned this, and among Peary admirers his Inuit wife and children are still regarded as skeletons best left in the closet of the polar night.

The relationship between Peary and "Ally," as he called her, was an interesting one, highly illustrative of his character. At first he was almost inclined to acknowledge her before the world—until members of the Peary Arctic Club made it clear that this wouldn't be tolerated. In one of his early books he published a photograph of her in the nude (she was young then and strikingly beautiful), an action that horrified his chief backer, Morris K. Jesup, a New York millionaire who had made a public career of prudery and used parts of his fortune in a campaign to stamp out "licentiousness." Peary never repeated the indiscretion.

His American wife, however, may have heard rumors, for she took passage on a supply ship without her husband's knowledge and made an unscheduled appearance in northwest Greenland. There, during his absence on a sledge journey, she met Allakasingwah, who by then could speak enough English to explain her relationship with Peary.

The two wives seem to have gotten along rather well and spent the winter together at Etah. Perhaps because she had a long time to think it over, and to get used to the idea of a polygamous relationship, the first Mrs. Peary kept quiet about the whole thing, the scandal that would have ended Peary's career in the United States was averted, and he was able to keep up the front of a respectable American marriage for the rest of his life. To reinforce this image, he always made a big thing of being photographed with wife and children during his arrivals and departures at New York or Boston.

Nearly all Peary's personal followers took common-law wives among the "Polar Eskimos." Matt Henson, his Negro servant, fathered a son in northern Greenland, and this Negro-Inuit halfbreed, an exceptionally strong and handsome man, was later attached to some of Bartlett's expeditions. But I have never been able to find evidence that Bartlett himself took advantage of the Inuit custom of sexual hospitality. He appears to have remained celibate in the Arctic—perhaps the only member of the Peary expeditions who did.

Just north of Etah, on the Canadian side of Smith Sound, is a small island with a point of land named Cape Sabine. The *Windward* managed with great difficulty to make her way across the ice-choked sound, here less than thirty miles wide, and around the cape, only to find Kane Basin, to the north, blocked with solid ice from shore to shore. They managed to get the ship into a small bay, just north of the cape. They still had three hundred miles to go to reach the north coast of Ellesmere—Peary's "Grant Land,"which he professed to believe was a separate island. But it was impossible to cover a single mile of that distance in that ship that year. A better ship might have wormed and battered her way along the coast a few miles farther to the north. The Windward was frozen in and snugged down for the winter. So Peary was forced to establish his southern base three hundred miles farther south than he intended, and though he seems not to have realized it, he was already defeated in his attempt to reach the pole before the end of the century.

Kane Basin is nearly always blocked with ice. Robeson Channel, the ten-mile-wide bottleneck connecting it to the Arctic Ocean, is always blocked. Getting north around Ellesmere from Cape Sabine means working your way for three hundred miles through a narrow lead of open water, often only a few feet wide, that develops along the east coast of Ellesmere in late August and early September when meltwater is pouring eastward into the sea from the mile-high glaciers inland.

On the Windward expedition, John Bartlett did not attempt this feat. Indeed, with his ship's twenty-five horsepower, it would have been useless. Only a properly powered ship, preferably with an ice-breaking hull, could hope to do it successfully.

Peary might have waited for summer and tried again to reach Fort

Conger by ship, but instead he kept teams of dogs and Inuit working all winter, sledging supplies northward to Fort Conger, still dreaming of an assault on the pole in 1899. He was spurred to superhuman—not to say foolhardy—efforts by the presence in Smith Sound that year of the world's greatest explorer, Otto Sverdrup, who had already drifted completely across the Arctic Ocean in the *Fram*.

Sverdrup had, by this time, contributed more than any man alive to knowledge of the Arctic and was, in the course of this trip, to map hundreds of thousands of square miles of unexplored territory. He wished Peary good luck and offered him any assistance in his power, but Peary had nightmares of Sverdrup's beating him to the pole. In fact, he needn't have worried. When Sverdrup found the route to the north blocked with ice, he turned to the unexplored west, the Canadian Arctic Archipelago and almost completed the mapping of it, discovering in the process the last *large* bodies of undiscovered land in the world, known now as the Sverdrup Islands. He missed just three of them—all comparatively small—and these were finally placed on the map by Stefansson, fifteen years later.

Sverdrup was the greatest contributor of his time not only to knowledge of the arctic land masses, but also to the nature of the Arctic Ocean itself. It was he who discovered it to be a true ocean, not a "Polar Sea," as Peary continued to call it to the end of his days. Sverdrup showed that it had an oceanic, or "abyssal," deep and demonstrated that the North Pole lies on a midocean plain under thousands of fathoms of water. Reaching this latitude, as a mere feat of endurance, when its nature and geography were already known, was of no interest to him whatever.

The presence of the *Fram*, a far better ship than his own, and of Sverdrup, whom he didn't for a moment underestimate, drove Peary to take unwarranted risks with his own life and the lives of others. He not only made sledge journeys of hundreds of miles in midwinter, but even continued to make them when there was no moonlight. In the Arctic you have the midday moon in winter just as you have the midnight sun in summer, and it gives enough light for working at all hours except for ten or twelve days a month. Peary drove himself and his Inuit and his dogs to work even during the ten to twelve days of darkness. He continued traveling, although the temperature dropped to —45. Some of the Inuit became stranded on the trail during the dark of the moon and barely escaped with their lives. Peary himself froze both his legs to the knee and spent months in a wooden shack at Fort Conger, more than two hundred miles from his ship, while his toes dropped off, joint by joint. When the sun returned, it became possible for the Inuit to carry him south, strapped to a sledge.

When at last he got back to the *Windward* in the spring of 1899, the surgeon amputated the few scraps that were left of his toes. A man without toes can walk, after a fashion and after retraining all the muscles of his legs and back. Peary had no time for this. Able to walk or no, he was determined to go on. By May, with the *Windward* still solidly frozen into the ice at Cape Sabine, he was sufficiently recovered to be taken on a sledge across the ice cap of northern Ellesmere Island to a point in the mountains above Greely Fjord from which he could finally see the ice of the Arctic Ocean to the north and west.

Perhaps he was still sick enough to suffer hallucinations, for it was on this journey that he reported the discovery of "Jesup Land," an illusory mountainous island lying to the northwest of Ellesmere in a place where there is nothing but an endless stretch of ice-covered ocean. He later tried to claim one of Sverdrup's discoveries, Axel Heiberg Island, as "Jesup Land," but it lies in a different direction from the land of his report, and the claim was rejected.

Peary spent four fruitless years on Ellesmere without ever organizing the advance on the pole which was the whole purpose of his expedition. Finally he was forced by lack of food and other supplies to abandon the attempt. He retired southward in 1902, defeated and crippled by the polar ice. Not even his most ardent supporter expected him to try again. But he had made at least one major discovery during the trip. He had discovered that young Robert Bartlett had the ability, if any man alive had it, to get him to the North Pole. He asked Bartlett to become the captain of a new ship on a new voyage into the arctic ice. Bartlett agreed, and together they planned both the type of ship and the route they would follow—northward through the narrow lead of water around the ice foot of Ellesmere and into the Arctic Ocean.

Bartlett laid down one condition. He must accompany Peary on the final sledge journey to the pole itself. Peary readily agreed to this, and Bob returned home, after four years in the Arctic, to tell his father, "On the next voyage, I'm going to the North Pole."

When Peary got back to civilization with his report of the discovery of Jesup Land, he found a further vexation awaiting him. While he was on Ellesmere Island, an Italian polar party, traveling north by sledge from the ice front near Franz Josef Land, had reached a new record latitude: 86°34´ north—a mere 236 miles from the pole itself. The race was truly, under way, and the prize might go to almost anyone, of any nationality, who happened to run into good luck and good weather and fairly smooth ice.

Peary immediately set about a campaign to raise the money to build a ship somewhat like the *Fram* only bigger, one that could withstand, if not actually navigate in, the polar pack.

Bob Bartlett had never been keen on the idea of a vessel that would simply ride up on the ice, when it tried to crush her, and sit there at the mercy of its drift until she was released months or years later. His idea was to build a steel-reinforced hull of enormous power and strength, backed by a powerful engine that could force the ship through all but the thickest ice sheets, thus giving her captain the means to batter his way farther north than any ship had managed to go before, under her own power.

In the end Peary settled for that kind of ship. The Fram had simply been frozen in and allowed to drift. She was designed for exactly that. The *Roosevelt* was not intended to be frozen in except as a last resort. She was to achieve by strength and brute force what no ship before her had ever done.

6

"... beyond human strength."

The *Roosevelt* was the only ship in history to clear Canadian customs "for the North Pole,"Bartlett's way of twisting the tail of fate—and in 1905, the year of her maiden voyage, the gods or the stars or whatever powers govern human fate were clearly against him.

The planning and engineering of the *Roosevelt* had been expert and thorough, but not the same can be said for her construction. There were hidden faults, even if she looked near-perfect. Though not a true icebreaker, she had sides sufficiently rounded to make it hard for an ice field to get a solid grip on her. The engines—still depending on coal fires and steam boilers—were powerful enough to butt through at least five or six feet of solid ice. She also had sails, so she could be steered, after a fashion, even with the rudder gone, and by using them to catch the wind alternately from side to side, she could be rocked out of an ice jam.

The ship was also extraordinarily strong, with massive crossbeams. But Bartlett immediately noted one major weakness: the huge coal-fired engine made it impossible to crossbrace the whole inside of the ship with wooden struts, as he wished to do. She was strong enough fore and aft, but a little weak amidships. Still, she was far better equipped to cope with the Arctic than anything he had sailed before. He assured Peary that he would take her right into the Arctic Ocean.

des. of ship

"That will depend on the ice," Peary pointed out.

"Damn the ice; I'll get her there," Bartlett promised.

They were obliged to do something spectacular on this trip. Peary's voyages, so far, had been spectacular failures, his "discovery" of the north coast of Greenland the only thing he had to show for a quarter of a century in the Arctic. His fiftieth birthday was only a few months off. He was permanently crippled and could hide his limp only during a short and painful walk. He was deeply in debt. His millionaire backers Morris Jesup and Thomas Hubbard had put up $50,000 each to help build the Roosevelt. They expected results for their money—at the very least to have the most northerly lands in the world named after them. George Crocker had given $50,000 to help finance the voyage, and other members of the Peary Arctic Club had given whatever they could spare. Peary had also borrowed to the limit on his own credit and that of his friends. Before the first Roosevelt voyage began, it had already cost more than half a million dollars at a time when a dollar was worth at least ten times what it is today.

Every man in the crew was a Newfoundlander and a veteran of the seal hunt—a far more dangerous job, Bartlett noted, than traveling over the polar pack. The explorers who were to act as leaders of the various ice parties, like Peary himself, went along strictly as passengers. Their job would begin after Bartlett and his crew had placed the *Roosevelt* farther north than any ship except the *Fram* had ever been before.

Taking a ship, no matter how well designed, into the arctic ice on her maiden voyage was a foolhardy thing to do. Every ship is liable to have flaws that become apparent only after she has been in use for some time. A year's voyaging in waters more friendly than those of Ellesmere Island would have been desirable. But they were in a hurry. The "discovery" of the North Pole was no longer a question of geography, science, or exploration. It was simply a sporting event, with the prize (glory, gold medals, book royalties, and big fees on the lecture circuit) going to the man who got there first.

Almost from the day they sailed, the *Roosevelt* appeared to be jinxed. They'd barely left Cape Breton when two of her boilers blew up, leaving her with one-third normal power. Miraculously, nobody was hurt in the explosion, and against all reason they decided to continue the voyage on the one remaining boiler. They hoisted all sails, and thenceforth used both sail and steam continuously.

Bartlett didn't spare the tough little ship. (He never spared any ship in his life. The way he treated ships was ruthless, almost savage. That was one reason Peary had chosen him to open "the American route to the Pole.") Taking final supplies at Etah, the earth's northernmost village, he stuck her nose into the ice of Kennedy Channel and began butting back and forth, hammering his way northward foot by foot.

He now began living in the crow's-nest, a barrel fixed at the head of the mainmast to give the navigator the broadest possible view of the ice field. It also gave some slight protection from the wind. From the crow's-nest the navigator would shout orders down to the bridge, where they would be relayed to the engine room and to the man at the wheel.

In this fashion he "scunned" the ship northward into Kane Basin, set up supply depots on the Ellesmere shore, and fought and ground his way through ice that was sometimes thirty feet thick into Robeson Channel (the narrow neck of water leading into the Arctic Ocean), now jammed from shore to shore with ice.

"It was a terrible fight," Bartlett admitted. "Day after day we thought the ice was going to crush the ship. It took us three weeks to fight our way from Etah to Cape Sheridan, and every day seemed to be the last of the voyage." The average distance made good was fifteen to sixteen miles a day—six tenths of a mile an hour. Ice conditions that year were no better than they had been in 1898, when the *Windward* had been stopped three hundred miles short of her goal. But they had arrived, by design, during the few weeks of late summer when the ice field loosened along the

Ellesmere ice foot and a lead of water, a few yards wide, opened there from time to time. Taking advantage of this, Bartlett wormed and battered his way through Robeson Channel and got into the harborless cove at Cape Sheridan (near the place where the Canadian base Alert is now) on the actual shore of the Arctic Ocean. He had done what he promised, in spite of the ship's lack of power, and had done it by September 5, just about the date originally planned. Here they would spend the winter, set up an advance base at Cape Columbia, two days by dog team to the northwest, and prepare for a multistaged journey over the sea ice toward the North Pole early the next spring.

At Cape Sheridan the *Roosevelt* was far from safe. Rafting sea ice came right into the cove where she lay and continually threatened to wreck her. September 16 was almost the last day of her life. Layer after layer of ice piled into the cove, driving irresistibly against the land. It caught the ship fore and aft, lifted her up, and heeled her over. It piled up against both sides and began to squeeze her like a nut in a nutcracker. Her deck bulged. Her propeller was tilted far out of the water. And then, when her last moment seemed to have arrived, the multiple ice sheets started to slide under her keel, to shatter and to splinter. As she was released, she regained her normal shape—the bulging deck sprang back into place, the cracked ribs straightened out. She leaked a little, but that could be repaired. It was about as narrow an escape as a ship could survive, but survive she did, and with only minor damage.

Peary had about sixty people—mostly Inuit—and about two hundred dogs, assembled at Cape Sheridan.* There was no way the *Roosevelt* could carry enough food to supply an expedition of this size even for one year, much less two. The plan had always been to live mainly by hunting. So they organized an absolutely ruthless slaughter of the Ellesmere Island game. That autumn they killed two hundred and forty musk ox and caribou—mostly musk ox—and so many walrus and polar bears that they simply stopped counting them. There were no inhabitants on Ellesmere Island and only the southern parts were even visited by the Greenland Inuit; the nearest Canadians were at Pond Inlet, six hundred miles away, so north Ellesmere was almost virgin territory where the herds of musk ox and caribou had slowly reached the maximum that the sparse soil and

---

* The records are maddeningly incomplete. It never occurred to them that anyone might want to know the names, or even the numbers, of the "Eskimos" who worked for them.

sun would support. For a year or two there would be seemingly limitless supplies of game. After that the animals might take a century to recover. So long as the light lasted, hunting parties scoured the land to the west and south, shooting everything that moved. Then Peary kept his people busy all winter sledging in supplies of meat and supplying the base at Cape Columbia from which the polar thrust would be made.

On February 19, while the cold of winter was still at its worst and the long night still unbroken by sunrise, Bartlett set out with the first sledges and the pioneer party of Inuit to cut a trail through the pressure ridges of the ice pack and build a sledge road toward the pole over which supply parties, and finally Peary himself, could travel. His job, now and always, was to break trail—to find the most direct route by careful navigation and literally to chop his way with picks and axes through the rough ice.

Two support parties followed, carrying supplies and building snowhouses. Finally Peary came along, four days behind Bartlett, riding on his sledge and carrying more supplies. He was the only one who rode a sledge and only because he had to. The two hundred pounds that he weighed, dressed in his furs, was dead weight that seriously reduced his chance of success. Over the trail that Bartlett had built for him, Peary was usually able to cover thirty or even forty miles a day, exceptionally fast for dog-team travel on sea ice.

Bartlett spent one hundred and twenty-one days on the ice of the Arctic Ocean that year, doing everything that a man could do to open the road to the pole. He himself admitted in the end that it was a task beyond human strength. He literally ran his dogs to death. He took chances that even the seasoned Inuit, with their happy-go-lucky attitude toward life, regarded as hair-raising. He sometimes had to shame them into going on—an easy task with an Inuk, to whom honor is dearer than life and ridicule deadlier than a bullet.

And it all went for nothing. The advance parties were brought to a standstill on the edge of the continental shelf, where the shore ice and the ocean ice tend to part because of an upwelling of water along the continental slope, forming what Bartlett called "the Big Lead," a name that has since stuck, in preference to Peary's more fanciful "Hudson River."

The Big Lead varied from a quarter of a mile to more than two miles wide. Patches of it often froze over, but the new ice tended to crack and part continually. It could be crossed from time to time on buckling young ice or on floating ice pans, but never with real safety. After they reached it, the advance parties spent six days there before getting a single komatik across. Then, with what looked like a clear route before them, they were pinned down by storms.

On April 21, two months and two days after his first thrust northward Bartlett reached latitude 85°12′. For practical purposes, a degree of latitude may be regarded as 69 statute miles, a minute as 1.15 miles. At this point, therefore, Bartlett was 331 miles from the pole. In two months of tremendous toil he had covered only 110 miles, not much more than two miles a day. At that rate of travel, reaching the pole would take another five and a half months, and there would be no way ever to get back.

Peary ordered him to return to land but decided to sledge farther north himself, not in any effort to reach the pole, for that was now completely out of the question, but to try for a latitude record. To beat the record set by the Italians, he would have to travel another hundred miles. Even that looked impossible, but if he got exceptionally good luck, fine weather, and smooth ice, he just might do it.

On this thrust, Peary took the greatest chances of his career. Normally a cautious man, this time he came close to risking everything. He turned back only when his dogs and Inuit were so close to exhaustion that it seemed doubtful if they could ever reach land. Most of his dogs by now were dead. He and his men ate most of the rest of them to keep alive on the return journey. They barely made it to the north coast of Greenland, where they were lucky enough to find and slaughter a herd of musk ox on the very day of their arrival, at a time when they were so close to starvation that they could not have survived another week.

Peary later claimed his "furthest north" on this dash—a latitude of 87°6′, just two hundred miles from the pole and thirty-six miles closer than the Italians—but the claim has been vigorously attacked by his critics. He offered no proof that he had reached this latitude—no depth sounding, no sighting for longitude, and above all, no record of magnetic deviation. Since no one can tell, in advance, what the magnetic deviation is going to be at any point previously unvisited on the earth's surface, this measurement (easily made by anyone with a compass, a watch, and a view of the sun) is of supreme importance in establishing that you have actually been where you say you were.

But whatever the merits of Peary's claim, no one should deny his courage or his tenacity. In 1906 he was defeated by the weather, by a series of storms, open water, and fast-drifting ice that carried him far to the eastward of his line of march. He was traveling over sea ice, with only a few days on land, from February 22 until he got back to the *Roosevelt* on June l. Anyone who could do this, and live for weeks on the carcasses of starving dogs, was no common imposter, as some critics claim, even if he was sometimes tempted to stretch his journeys by a few miles or to sight new lands that he couldn't be completely certain were really there.

Peary's most notorious "discovery," a place he called Crocker Land for a member of his club who had donated $50,000 to the venture, was made that summer. He left the *Roosevelt* on June 2 with the specific purpose of exploring a stretch of previously untraveled coast—a hundred miles of the north shore of Ellesmere Island—whose capes and bays were to be named after his financial backers.

Peary's detractors have often discussed this practice as though it were mean and even contemptible. It was, however, straight business and his only means of financing his expeditions. If he was ever to raise the money for another—and he was already planning to try again—he must immortalize the armchair explorers of the Peary Arctic Club by writing their names across the map. He was by no means alone in this practice. The great Sverdrup, a few years earlier, had named the Canadian arctic islands he discovered after a bunch of brewers and burghers who had backed him. Stefansson, a few years later, when bankrolled by the Canadian Government, felt obliged to name the world's last-discovered lands after a group of obscure and venal Tory politicians in Ottawa.

Peary sledged along the whole north coast of Ellesmere and crossed the ice to the north cape of Axel Heiberg Island. Thence, looking northwest he reported the mountains of a new land, not a small island but something that filled the horizon—clear and unmistakable icy peaks rising against the northern sky.

If Crocker Land was not an honest error, then it was a deliberate fraud. Unfortunately, the evidence for a deliberate fraud is extremely strong, though not conclusive. Peary left no record of the Crocker Land sighting in the Ellesmere Island cairns erected a day or two after the discovery. He did not mention Crocker Land in the report he cabled to the United States on November 2, 1906. He did not mention it to Bartlett, or to any other member of the expedition, until long after the expedition was over. And he did not mention it in any of his public appearances between then and February 1907. His two diaries, which should have included sightings for his "furthest north" and an entry recording the Crocker Land discovery, vanished mysteriously from among his papers. Most damning of all, in the cairn he erected on June 30, he reported, "a good view of the northern horizon" from Cape Hubbard, as he called it, but said nothing of the land he later claimed to be visible from that point. The evidence is therefore strong that Peary invented Crocker Land after he got back to the United States and had to face George Crocker, who had put up just as much money as Hubbard or Jesup but had been left without a cape to call his own.

In spite of the damning nature of all this, Peary may not have been guilty of a total fabrication. He may have truly believed that he saw *something* in the far distance on two separate sightings to the northwest. If he was less than completely sure about what he saw—clouds or mist or pressure ridges looking like ice-covered mountains, an arctic mirage that could translate a pressure ridge into an island or even a continent— he might delay reporting it, hoping for a clearer, less ambiguous sight. And then, pressed by the urgent need to satisfy his backers, he might have gradually infused the uncertain sighting with greater and greater certainty until he was convinced, himself, that he saw far more than he did and persuaded himself of the certainty of land to the northwest of Ellesmere, where there is nothing, either to the north or the west, for more than a thousand miles. Such, in my own view, is the probable origin of his mythical Crocker Land.

On July 4, while Peary was still on his way back from Axel Heiberg Island, Bartlett broke out of the ice trap that had held the *Roosevelt* fast

for eleven months. He rounded Cape Sheridan and bulled his way into
Robeson Channel, seeking a berth from which he could head south a
month later, when they'd be ready to leave for home. He sent a dog team
with a letter to Peary, instructing him to join the ship at Fort Conger, in
Kane Basin.

Only twenty miles south of the cape, however, the sea ice closed in
from the eastward and forced the *Roosevelt* against the rocks. Again it
rafted up her sides, tilted her stern skyward, and went crashing under her
keel. This time, however, she did not get off as easily as the year before.
A huge rafting pan passed under her counter, tore off the sternpost,
demolished the rudder, broke two of the four propeller blades, and tore
a hole in her bottom "almost big enough for a small boy to crawl
through." Bartlett, going below to assess the damage, was appalled to see
daylight through a crack that had opened along the whole length of her
skeg. When the pressure eased, after about fifteen minutes, she closed up
a little. Then he roared for all hands to get busy with oakum, rags, and
cement before the ice should let her settle into the sea and sink. They
worked furiously as she was gradually released, and by the time she was
back into the water, they had stuffed a cubic yard of rags and oakum and
a full barrel of cement into the hole. Even then she leaked so much that
they had to run the pumps continually to keep her afloat. They then
rebuilt the rudder.

Back in the water but still jammed by the ice, she drifted southward
through Robeson and Kennedy channels even more slowly than she had
worked her way northward the year before. Peary followed the Ellesmere
ice shelf southward and rejoined her while she was still solidly frozen in.
Otherwise, he would have had to rejoin her at Cape Sabine. The battle
with the ice went on till August 27, when she got into Kane Basin and
was temporarily released. Two days later, she was jammed again and
remained jammed until September 5. Then for nine days they inched
southward a mile or two a day.

By September 14 they were near Cape Sabine, where the *Windward*
had spent more than three years. The three-hundred-mile voyage had
taken more than ten weeks. By now the new ice was increasing at the rate
of almost an inch a day and was so thick close to the shore that the

Roosevelt had to butt her way through it.

She got into Smith Sound on September 16 and sailed into Etah harbor that night, after seventy-five days of continuous battle with the ice field. It is doubtful if any ship in history had taken such a beating and survived. Bartlett beached her sternfirst in Etah Fjord, and between tides he fitted a new rudder, built a new sternpost, and rebolted the remaining propeller blades.

He described her in his log as "a complete wreck" but a wreck that he intended to sail home for all that. Every few hours, on the way south through Kennedy Channel, he had gone to his cabin to make a "final entry" in the log. For two and a half months he had been "battling the ice pack in a sinking ship." No wonder he believed, after that, that he could get her back to New York on will power alone.

On the evening of September 20, they steamed out of Etah Fjord with their second jury rudder, half a propeller, and the hole in the bottom covered with a canvas patch. Their one remaining boiler was leaky and had to be patched to make it hold steam pressure.

They spent six more days on the west Greenland coast, delivering members of the expedition to their various home villages and butting through the ever-increasing ice before they got into completely clear water, still north of the Arctic Circle, and headed for home, southward across Melville Bay.

The *Roosevelt* now ran into a series of gales—normal enough, so far north in October—and on the sixth their third rudder was carried away by the sea. In such a storm, no jury rudder could be fitted; so Bartlett rigged the mizzen boom over the stern, weighted the end with a kedge anchor that also served as a blade, and worked it with ropes and pulleys fastened to the deck winches. They steered with this amazing rig for two days until the sea went down and they had a jury rudder built—their fourth. Then they ran out of coal.

By now, however, they were off the coast of Labrador, and there was a chance they might be able to buy fuel. Limping into Hebron, the most northerly permanent settlement on that coast, they found not a lump of coal in the place. The Inuit, however, had laid in a good supply of green spruce, cut far to the south in Okak Bay, and had surplus whale blubber and seal oil. So they bought three scowloads of wood and as much blubber and oil as the people could spare. With this mixture they managed to fire their boiler and keep up steam, and so they limped along the coast as far as Nain, where they could buy all the wood they wanted.

Running on wood and blubber, they got to Hopedale, where a coal store had once stood, though it was now empty. A lot of coal, however, had fallen through the floor into a pit beneath. They salvaged it, lump by lump, until they had a total of seven tons. At Hawk's Harbour they bought two more tons. And this, supplemented by wood and blubber, took them as far as Battle Harbour, into which dangerous little strait— a mere open channel between islands—they limped on November 2, and sent word of their discoveries and their failure to the world by cable.

At Battle Harbour they bought forty tons of coal but were pinned down by a ten-day gale of such violence that it broke their main anchor and tore their mooring lines to shreds. They managed to save the ship only by mooring her to the rocks with chains.

On November 13, the wind dropped enough for them to get out of the Battle Harbour channel, but they made only four miles headway that day against a furious sea with a head wind and blinding snowstorm. Two days later they made it through the Straits of Belle Isle into the Gulf of St. Lawrence and coasted southward along the western shore of Newfoundland. Halfway along that shore their fuel ran out again, but they got a few tons of coal at Sandy Point in St. George's Bay (rowing it off in boats because the water there was too shallow to approach shore). Then a few more tons at Port aux Basques enabled them to reach Sydney, Cape Breton, where coal, if little else, was in limitless supply.

Here Peary, thankful to see the last of the Roosevelt for that year, boarded a train for New York, leaving Bartlett in sole charge of the wreck. He decided to take the ship through Great Bras d'Or and Bras d'Or Lake and St. Peter's Canal to the southeast corner of Cape Breton Island and the open sea—a lovely trip for a yacht. But trying to get into the locks at St. Peter's without an adequate rudder, they ran up on a mudbank, crashed through a fence, and chased a girl and a cow out of a field. Fortunately, the Roosevelt had powerful deck winches. They located a stout tree on the opposite bank, attached a cable, and winched themselves off.

They then passed safely through the locks, only to run aground once more on a shoal between St. Peter's and Isle Madame, where shoals are rife and tides run high. Bartlett blamed this stranding on faulty buoying of the channel. Be that as it may, the tide was just beginning to flow, and at high tide she floated off without damage.

Meanwhile, the boiler had sprang another leak, so the engine was useless. They tried to get into Halifax for repairs on sails alone but were driven offshore by another gale. Two days later they managed to make port at Selburne, in southern Nova Scotia, where the boiler was patched well enough to keep up steam.

"We practically drifted across the Bay of Fundy," Bartlett admitted, and fetched up on the Maine shore—literally. The tide, bad luck to it, ran faster than the crippled ship. She lost steerage way and drifted aground on a mudbank.

Once again, with kedges and winches, they got her off. It was the final mishap of the voyage. On December 24, against all the laws of probability, the *Roosevelt* crept into the mouth of the Hudson River and dropped her one remaining anchor off the port of New York.

"I went to my bunk and passed into blissful unconsciousness," Bartlett wrote later. It had taken him ninety-nine days to get his wreck home from Etah, a hundred and seventy-four days from the time she had been almost torn in two by the ice—a nightmare voyage of six months' duration that must surely surpass anything ever attempted for sheer stubbornness and refusal to accept defeat. Any time after he raised the coast of Labrador he could have wintered the ship in fair safety, and they could have made their way home in coastal vessels and trains. Then, in the spring, she could have been towed to a safe port for repairs. That is what almost any other captain in the world would have done. Not Bartlett. He had to attempt the "impossible." And the fantastic luck that seemed to follow him through all his misfortunes held once again—they all got through it alive.

He slept fourteen hours a day for a week. During the same week he attended nightly dinners and then sneaked off for extra meals of steak and onions all by himself. In seven days he was back to normal and heading for Newfoundland to get ready for the 1907 seal hunt.

Peary got the Hubbard gold medal for the voyage. Bartlett got a twenty-dollar gold piece from Morris Jesup. He kept it for a good-luck charm, and half a century later it was still among his souvenirs at Brigus.

7

"I don't know, perhaps I cried a little."

After the failure of 1906, the Roosevelt had to be practically rebuilt and a new expedition fitted out. Peary published a book, Nearest the Pole, hoping to earn as much as $100,000 in royalties, but it was a flop. People wanted to read about success, not about heroic attempts that failed. Morris Jesup, always the most generous of his backers, died. The financial outlook was so bleak that Peary asked Bartlett to come to New York in the spring of 1907 and join him in a campaign to raise money for another voyage.

"I knocked at the doors of political leaders and millionaires," Bartlett said afterward. "I was rebuffed, laughed at, offered jobs, sympathized with and in a hundred ways resisted . . it was a glorious fight; but we failed—that year at least."

He packed up and went back to seal hunting. He had sailed with his father the spring of 1907, and they had returned with a bumper load of pelts. But the spring of 1908 merely added to his woes. He was given command of the *Leopard*, the auxiliary barkentine that had almost always been commanded by a Bartlett, and he sailed from St. John's for the Gulf of St. Lawrence, an area where his father and uncles had always done well with seals. Sealing ships going to and from the Gulf always take the southern route around Cape Race. That year the ice off Newfoundland's east coast was heavy. Instead of staying in the ice and trying to work southward through leads, Bob tried to do with the *Leopard* what he had done three years before with the *Roosevelt*: follow the lane of water that is often to be found close inshore. It was a tight squeeze in many places. The winds were easterly. The ship, like most ships of her age, was underpowered. Near Cappahayden his luck ran out and he was forced on the rocks. At the time there was a heavy swell running from storms behind the ice field, and within a few hours the *Leopard* was a total loss.

Fortunately, Bartlett and his men were able to land without difficulty. They suffered no loss of life and little loss of gear, but their hope for a profitable spring was wiped out. Two days after sailing, they were back in St. John's, penniless.

The spring of 1908 was the rock bottom of Bob Bartlett's early career. From March to June he stayed in Brigus and moped about, doing nothing.

"Rarely have I been so depressed as I was in those months," he said. He had failed both as an explorer and a seal hunter. It seemed doubtful that he'd get another sealing ship, having lost his vessel through an error of judgment, and it seemed unlikely that the money could be found for another massive assault on the polar ice. Then the unexpected happened. A cable arrived from Peary, and within two days Bartlett was assembling a crew to take to New York to get the *Roosevelt* ready for sea.

On arrival he found her still underfitted because Peary had been unable to raise the funds to equip her properly. The voyage was going to be run on "faith, hope and credit." Success would bring millions of dollars from the lecture circuit. Failure would mean financial ruin. It was the gamble of a lifetime.

It was already June when Peary made up his mind to sail that year. It took a month to get the ship ready, Thomas B. Hubbard putting up most of the money. They sailed from Oyster Bay on July 7, 1908, President Theodore Roosevelt, with wife and children, coming to see them off. At Sydney they were joined by the *Erik*, a Newfoundland sealer, carrying eight hundred tons of coal.

The ships next rendezvoused at Etah, where the *Erik* discharged and headed south. Then the *Roosevelt*, carrying besides her crew and Peary's party of explorers, seventy-six Inuit,* two hundred forty-six dogs, with seventy tons of mostly rotten whale meat to feed them, stuck her bow once more into the ice of Kane Basin and Robeson Channel.

On September 5 they dropped anchor at Cape Sheridan, three years to the day after anchoring there for the first time. It had been a comparatively easy passage, with no damage to the ship, for the ice was looser than usual that summer. Nevertheless, they quickly emptied the ship of her supplies and stored them ashore, in case she might be sunk by rafting ice.

Almost at once they began moving stores overland to Cape Columbia, ninety miles northwest. They planned to keep a road open to this jumping-off point all winter, to be ready for the sledge journey toward the pole by late February, when the first daylight returned.

Earlier expeditions had spent the long polar night, when the sun never rose, in quarters either on ship or in roughly built houses ashore. The expeditions led by Peary were the first to make regular winter sledge journeys.

Arctic night (often incorrectly referred to as a six months'night by southern writers) is not as dark as you might imagine. Apart from the long twilight of some weeks' duration at the beginning and the end of it there are almost a hundred days of bright moonlight in the dark period between dusk and dawn. Bartlett described it thus:

"You know the monthly moon rises in the arctic above the horizon. . . it goes around in a big spiral until it reaches its point of maximum declination. This takes about a week. Then it starts down again. This takes nearly another week. So every month there is a lot more moonlight than we have down here.

---

* Bartlett's and Peary's accounts both refer to "forty-nine Eskimos," employed by the expedition. For some reason, the seventeen women, who worked even harder than the men, didn't count. There were also ten children, who kept the camps supplied with fresh water and did other chores.

"In this moonlight Peary kept all hands sledging and hunting. During the dark days we had all we could do to get our gear cleaned up and in shape before the next moon came. Naturally with such a routine the winter flew by. The men kept in fine physical shape and spirits and we gathered more and more fresh meat and skins for the stiff spring dash to the north."

Peary's komatiks were built by the Inuit, but not from local materials. They were made of wood and steel that he brought north on his ships. With these critical materials, always in short supply in the Arctic, they were able to build longer sledges with wider runners than those they built for themselves. Peary's komatiks had a load capacity of six hundred and fifty pounds each. They were hauled by teams of ten dogs with food for fifty days. If no new supplies of meat were expected during a journey, that meant each sledge had to carry five hundred pounds of dog food, leaving a scant hundred and fifty pounds of payload. This narrow margin between what the sledges could carry and what the dogs needed to keep going explains the massive size of the Peary expeditions. Not until six years later was Stefansson to demonstrate that you could get by with lighter loads, trusting to the resources of the Arctic Ocean to feed yourself and your dogs at least part of the time. Peary always assumed that everything you used had to be hauled from a base on shore.

Bartlett left the ship for Cape Columbia on February 15, 1909, accompanied by eight komatiks and fifty-six dogs, instead of the standard eighty. Since the first ninety miles would be overland, the sledges were lightly loaded, and some of the teams could be sent back to the ship for more supplies. On arrival at the cape, he departed northward, leading the first party on the first stage of the polar journey. Meanwhile Peary, leaving seven days after Bartlett, had joined him at the cape. Bartlett's departure was February 28. He recorded a clear day with little wind and a temperature of —45° ("fifty below zero." Most temperature records given in Bartlett's accounts are probably only estimates. Except in rare cases they appear in round figures, such as this).

"We were the pioneer party," Bartlett said. "Our work was to set the course, break the trail, and gauge the distance for the main party."

A day on a polar "dash" began with tea and pemmican at 2 to 3 A.M.

There was, of course, no night. But Bartlett continued to live by the clock and to keep something like a regular twenty-four-hour schedule. If the weather was clear, they traveled by the sun, which was due south at midday, due north at midnight, and the appropriate number of degrees east or west at all hours between. So long as the sun was visible it was not too difficult to head true north. If the sun was obscured, he must rely on a compass, which in those latitudes could indicate only a very rough and approximate course. At Cape Columbia they were well to the north of the magnetic pole, in a place where the approximate compass variation was 180°. In other words, the south pole of the compass pointed more or less north, but it changed from day to day, and it was impossible to rely on compass courses without frequent sun sights to correct them.

With compass, chronometer, and sextant, Bartlett laid out his course and stuck to it as closely as ice conditions would permit. However, the ice was neither smooth nor continuous. Even far beyond the edge of the continental shelf open water was occasionally found, and pressure ridges were frequent, making detours necessary. If the horizon was clear enough to do so, he always took a noon sight with the sextant not only because this was the easiest way to compute latitude accurately, but also because the sun was then a little higher above the horizon than at other times. Even though it rose only a few degrees in its circle around the sky, this was enough, at noon, to overcome some of the problem of refraction that tends to displace the sun's image from its true position and consequently to give a false reading, one of the major navigation problems of high latitudes.

He and the Inuit in the pioneer party had to make a passable trail for the other parties following. They had to cut their way over pressure ridges and rough ice, leveling the track sufficiently for the heavily laden komatiks that followed. They also had to mark the trail with flags so that the supply teams could find their way out and back without navigation.

As Bartlett's supplies were used up, he received fresh ones from the following parties, who had left land later and traveled faster because the marked route had been built for them. These parties unloaded food and fuel at igloos built on the ice, thus creating a supply chain for the return of the pioneer party and for Peary's sledge team during its "dash" out and back. Then, with nearly empty komatiks, the supply parties returned rapidly to land.

Bartlett's progress was slow and arduous—crawling rather than dashing. Over a period of a month, even while working eighteen to twenty hours out of every twenty-four, he barely averaged ten miles a day. The following parties had it easier, of course; even so, the trail tended to drift and they were sometimes stopped by open water.

As Bartlett approached the center of the Arctic Ocean, a month after leaving land, he was hampered further by a southward drift of the ice. This was not unexpected. The wreckage of the *Jeannette*, picked up off southern Greenland three years after she was crushed north of Siberia, and the subsequent drift of the *Fram* had demonstrated that a current flows across the Arctic Ocean, northward toward the pole on the Siberian side and southward toward Greenland on the Canadian side. This drift could be computed at about two miles a day, so that a day's journey northward over the ice was lengthened by that amount.

The ice, however, got smoother, as if to compensate for the drift. As land was left far behind and the turbulence caused by the continental shelf lost its effect, the traveling became easier. The pole was more or less "in sight."

Bartlett, by now was a thoroughly experienced navigator. Peary, though he knew how to read latitude from a sextant, was not. It is doubtful if he could make a reading for longitude at all. Otherwise he would not have become so hopelessly lost in 1906, when he missed his route by twenty degrees and landed in Greenland, all the time thinking he was heading for Ellesmere Island.

The captain's first responsibility was to be absolutely certain of his position at all times. As you near the pole, navigation becomes more and more tricky, a compass useful only for measuring magnetic deviation. Frequent sextant sights are vital, and you must steer by the sun alone. As you approach 90° N., longitude and latitude become equally important. If you know from the chronometer what hour it is, and the exact bearing of the sun from the pole at that hour, then you can lay out a straight course northward. Without this knowledge there is no way of knowing if you are heading for the pole or for some other point to one side or the other of it, or even directly away from it; 90° N. was one of the most difficult spots on earth to locate by instruments. Stars, of course, were no help at that time of year since the daylight made them invisible. The only reference point was the sun, which was frequently bedeviled by mist and atmospheric refraction.

This, at least, was the situation in Bartlett's day. Since then, instruments for continuous polar location have been developed. But in 1909, only a master mariner with a thorough knowledge of his instruments, and practice of reading his position on the earth's surface from the sky, could navigate out of sight of land on the frozen Arctic Ocean without the near certainty of getting lost. This is not true of any other ocean in the world, where compass bearings are always reasonably correct and need at most to be checked at long intervals. In Bartlett's day, the magnetic variations in the Arctic were unknown, and even the position of the magnetic pole (which shifts constantly) was uncertain.

Bartlett's second job, cutting trail, was even more difficult. It took courage to face open leads and unknown ice conditions in a region where no one had ever traveled before. It also took tenacity and extraordinary physical stamina to fight your way forward foot by foot and build a trail day after day at a rate of no more than half a mile an hour. Fortunately, he had all these qualities in generous amounts, as well as long intimacy with ice fields.

Following immediately behind Bartlett was George Borup, with three Inuit and four dog teams, packing supplies. Borup, a college boy from Yale, was ordered to make only three marches along Bartlett's trail, then stash his supplies and return for a second load.

Similar parties were led, at one-day intervals, by Peary's Negro servant Matt Henson, who had been driving dogs for many years; by Ross Marvin, who was a Cornell mathematics professor; by Dr. J. W. Goodsell; and by Donald B. MacMillan, then a high-school teacher, later to lead his own expeditions and to gain fame as an explorer.

Last of all came Peary, riding his komatik with his Inuit driver, accompanied by other Inuit and dog teams carrying supplies.

"There followed a month of terrible labor for all hands," Bartlett recalled. "Each unit had to work out and back over a broken trail...keeping

Peary with his best dogs and Eskimos fairly well in the rear. This put the leader in touch with the units that had gone back to land for more supplies and also with units ahead of him who were breaking trail."

By March 14, after a week's delay caused by storms and open leads, Peary was heading northward along Bartlett's route, and the support parties began returning. First to turn back was Dr. Goodsell, from an estimated position 84°29′ N. Next went MacMillan, with two badly frozen heels, from approximately the same position. Then, on March 20, Borup turned back from 85°23′ N. Goodsell, MacMillan, and Borup were all on their first arctic expedition. Their ability to drive dogs and cross sea ice had been learned in the five months between their arrival at Cape Sheridan and their departure from Cape Columbia.

On March 26 Ross Marvin turned back from 86°38′ N. Because he was a civil engineer and a certified navigator, he made a signed statement to the effect that he had taken latitude readings and confirmed this position. During his last three marches, he had averaged sixteen and two-thirds nautical miles a day—about eighteen land miles, better than average for arctic ice.

Marvin was a driver and a martinet. He never got back to land. His death came about because of a fundamental failure to understand the Inuit. He treated his Inuit dog drivers as though they were lowly servants back in the United States. Inuit are used to independence and do not make good menials. The particular people with whom Marvin had to deal, the most northerly Inuit on earth, had not been exposed for very long to the white man's oddities.

His chief driver was a man named Kudlukto, who was assisted by a boy named Inugeeto, a cousin of Kudlukto's—"cousin," to an Inuk, meaning any relative, by blood, marriage, or adoption, not so close as a brother, son, or nephew.

The boy had been walking for many hours, chasing the dog team; he was near exhaustion and asked to be allowed to ride on the komatik. Kudlukto saw no reason why he shouldn't—the dogs were reasonably fresh and the load light. But Marvin refused categorically to allow it. To Marvin, coming from a people who admired the Spartans and believed that harshness was good for the young, this seemed natural enough. To

Kudlukto, coming from a people who treat youngsters with universal kindness and indulgence, it seemed like senseless cruelty. He began to gesture and insist, in his own language, on the boy's right to ride the sled. Marvin shook his head adamantly. Kudlukto became more excited, and when Marvin refused to give way, he grabbed a gun from the komatik and shot him. Then he pushed the body out on the young ice of a recently frozen lead, where it would soon break through and sink, and motioned the boy to climb on board the sledge.

When he met MacMillan on his return to the ship he reported, sadly, that Marvin had fallen through the ice and drowned. But about fifteen years later, when he became a Christian, he confessed the killing to a missionary, and the true story came out in all its details. Still later, Inugeeto told the story to MacMillan, but by that time Kudlukto was dead and beyond the reach of the white man's vengeance.

Peary and Henson, with seven sledges and dog drivers, now followed Bartlett's trail to his last camp, fifteen miles beyond Marvin's. They arrived just as Bartlett was ready to depart. Next day they took up his trail again and caught up with him six hours later. He had made camp at a point well beyond 87° N., one hundred and fifty miles short of the pole, fifty miles past the latitude claimed by Peary in 1906.

Bartlett still believed that he was going to the pole and knew for sure that he could get there. It was not until the next day that he learned Peary was ordering him back and taking Matt Henson instead on the final leg of the journey.

His description of his bitter disappointment (suppressed in later accounts) was poured out to a New York *Herald* reporter immediately after his return:

"I really didn't think I would have to go back....Then the Commander said I must go back—that he had decided to take Matt Henson....It was a bitter disappointment. I got up early the next morning while the rest were asleep, and started north alone. I don't know, perhaps I cried a little. I guess perhaps I was just a little crazy then. I thought that perhaps I could walk on the rest of the way alone. It seemed so near.

"Here I had come thousands of miles and it was only a little more than a hundred more to the pole." †

"The Commander figured on five marches more, and it seemed as if I could make it alone even if I didn't have any dogs or food or anything. I felt so strong I went along five miles or so, and then I came to my senses and knew I must go back."

If Peary, at this point, really intended to go on to the pole, then sending Bartlett back was the greatest mistake of his life. He later Invented various reasons for breaking faith with the man who had made the whole " dash" possible:

1. Henson, being a Negro, lacked the "daring and initative" of "my Anglo-Saxon friends." So it would be dangerous to send him back at the head of a party. (Bartlett, presumably, was an honorary Anglo-Saxon, even though he claimed to be of Spanish descent and looked like a Basque.)

2. He didn't want to "share" the pole with another white man.

3. Bartlett was a Newfoundlander, not an American, and he wanted the achievement of the pole to be an all-American one. (The four Greenlanders didn't count because they were"Eskimos.")

4. This had been the plan all along, and it was dangerous to change it.

It is worth nothing that Bartlett had no knowledge of any such plan. He had not only exacted a promise from Peary, at the beginning of their association, that he would be a member of the final polar party, but declared that Peary had promised him the same thing again at the start of the 1909 expedition.

His words to Theodore Roosevelt on departure, "Its ninety or nothing," confirm that he believed, then, that he was going to the pole

In the books that they eventually published, both Bartlett and Peary gloss over the quarrel that they had on April 1, 1909. Their accounts read as though they parted in the best of spirits; Bartlett, at worst, a little depressed. But the newspaper accounts that were closest to the event describe Bartlett as "arguing, begging, almost quarrelling" with Peary, before starting for Cape Columbia.

Next day, as Bartlett said, he left before Peary or Henson was awake.

---

† It was 150 miles, not "a little more than a hundred," but perhaps Bartlett was thinking in nautical, rather than statute, miles. The camp was 134 nautical miles from the pole.

He was now traveling farther north than any man had been before, or claimed to have been. Soon he turned around and went back to camp, where he found Peary and Henson awake and preparing for the last stage of the journey.

Peary's decision that he needed his valet more than his navigator on the last stage of his journey handed his critics their most powerful weapon. They said in 1909, and still say today, that he did not want a competent navigator along to report his real position because he already knew that the pole was out of his reach.

Bartlett never made any such criticism. He never criticized any superior in his life. He not only supported Peary's claims but professed to admire him in every respect and continued to do so to the end of his life. Whatever his other faults, Peary seems to have been a man who inspired confidence and loyalty in all his lieutenants.

That morning Bartlett reached what he believed to be 88° N. but was unable to confirm it with a sextant reading. He had earlier established a reading of 87°48´, then went another five nautical miles to get beyond the eighty-eighth parallel. He was never to know the exact position that he reached, however, because on turning back to his last camp, he discovered that it had drifted southward a mile and a half to 87°46´ 49". (Readings for "seconds" are said to be meaningless at this latitude because of the low angle of the sun, even at noon, and the effect of refraction of the atmosphere. Bartlett here gave the exact reading he obtained, not insisting on its absolute accuracy.)

Then he turned back for Cape Columbia. His estimate of the time it would take Peary to reach the pole was optimistic—eight days—but much less optimistic than Peary's own. To fulfill his schedule, Peary would need to make good an average of thirty miles a day over ice where no trail had been broken and against a southward drift of at least two miles daily and, more likely, three or four, judging by Bartlett's readings.

Peary had Henson and four Inuit, forty dogs, five komatiks, and, by stretching it to the limit and eating their dogs, enough food to return to land—but just enough, if everything went exactly right.

Bartlett's 87°48´ was the highest *confirmed* latitude ever reached by a human being in the Arctic until aircraft took over the job of exploration a generation later. How much farther than this Peary may have gone nobody knows, though opinions on the matter are extremely heated. For any claim he made after Bartlett turned south, there is only his unsupported word, without the evidence of any kind of geophysical readings. Not only did he lack a confirming observation for latitude, but he offered no supporting data. His original diary disappeared, as his original papers covering critical points of his career had an unfortunate habit of doing. His original sextant readings, if he ever made any, also disappeared. He gave no depth soundings except to report that at one place he had failed to find bottom at fifteen hundred fathoms. There was nothing new in this, since Sverdrup had already demonstrated the existence of an abyssal deep in the polar region. He reported no magnetic variations, either at the pole or at any point on his march, and Admiral Byrd was forced to write to Bartlett many years later, asking what compass variation Peary had "used" on his journey to the pole. The compass variations, which would have been childishly simple to do and could not have been faked without grave risk, would have established his claim beyond reasonable dispute.

The one fact that no one has ever disputed, in the midst of all this mess, is that Bartlett did what he said he did. He opened the road across the Arctic Ocean to a point one hundred and fifty miles from the pole, then unwillingly turned back for land.

If he, rather than Peary, had been leading the expedition, or if Peary had been willing to direct operations from shore, Bartlett would certainly have reached the pole. He was not only much younger and stronger than Peary, but he was able to walk every step of the way. Peary, with both his feet crippled, had to ride most of the way on a sledge. (Hensen reported he rode *all* the way on his return from the pole.) He thus represented two hundred pounds of dead weight, more than a full payload for one of his komatiks—weight that should have been replaced by supplies. If Bartlett, standing at the eighty-eighth parallel on April 1, 1909, had had, instead of his crippled commander, an extra two hundred pounds of pemmican and biscuit (enough to last a party of six men an additional sixteen days), he could have gone on to the pole in complete safety, taken all the time he could use about collecting scientific data, and returned at leisure, with enough supplies to last another six weeks if he needed them.

That was what might have been. What actually happened was something quite other than that. The journey back took him eighteen days of some of the hardest going in his life.

"It was drive her, boy, drive her!" he wrote to MacMillan. In his book, *The Log of Bob Bartlett*, published in 1928, he wrote: "I had a rough time before I reached land. We lost the trail in drifting snow, and I fell through young ice and nearly drowned. It was about 32 degrees below zero. The natives hauled me out and rolled me up in a musk ox robe. I was almost paralyzed with cold before I got my garments on. Luckily, we were near an igloo. So I came out of the jam without serious damage."

I do not intend to review at length the evidence with respect to Peary's claim to have reached the pole, except to say there is none. The job of analysis has been done thoroughly by others, and his claim shown to be of no value except to those who wish to take it on faith.

According to Peary, he spent thirty hours at the pole itself. Matt Henson confirmed that they did indeed spend thirty hours in camp somewhere or other, just before starting south on April 7 or 8. (Dates no longer meant anything; the sun was always the same distance above the horizon; there were no days or nights.) Assuming all this to be correct, Peary was eight or nine days behind Bartlett when he turned back. Add the eighteen days that it took Bartlett to reach land, and Peary's estimated time of arrival would have been thirty-five days after he and Bartlett parted at the eighty-eighth parallel. That is to say, he "should" have got back to land around May 5. Instead, he arrived at land on April 22 and was at Cape Columbia April 23, thirteen days sooner than should have been possible had he actually gone to the pole. A reasonable estimate, therefore, is that he stopped about six days' travel short of the pole, eighty to ninety miles. That may seem like a small distance, after a lifetime of effort, but with the breaking and drifting ice and rising temperatures that lay between Peary and land, and his critical shortage of food, it was the difference between life and death. If he had pushed forward across the trackless waste of ice, he could, indeed, have reached the pole. But he would never have been heard from again.

8

"...a gold brick...."

When Peary got back to the Roosevelt, Bartlett met him with the words: "I congratulate you, sir, on having reached the North Pole."

Peary said nothing. He went to his cabin and scarcely spoke to Bartlett or anyone else for several days. He still had not made up his mind exactly what he was going to claim. Would the world believe, without supporting data, that he'd actually reached the pole? Had the time out and back been long enough to make it sound plausible?

Bartlett's words probably had something to do with strengthening a half-formed resolve. If this man, who knew more about the difficulties than anybody else, who had come so close to doing it himself, believed that Peary had done it, then surely everybody else would believe it too.

To MacMillan, then across the channel in Greenland, he sent an ambiguous message: "Northern trip entirely satisfactory." That left him room to retreat. If he had already decided on the date, and firmly resolved to claim the pole, he would have written, "Reached pole April 6. All well," or something of that sort. "Entirely satisfactory" might mean only that he had reached farthest north, which indeed he had and returned safely.

After that he said nothing more about the pole to anybody for a month. He stayed in his cabin, perhaps working on his papers, and, to everyone's surprise, he gave no orders for a move southward. The original plan was to start south as early as the ship could be broken out of her berth in the ice. Peary had left word with the mate, a Newfoundlander named Gushue, that if he and Bartlett had not returned by June 1, they were to be considered lost, and Gushue was to begin working the ship southward. Now, instead, Peary laid out additional work for the entire expedition for the summer—geological and tidal surveys and a line of depth soundings stretching out into the ocean.

By the end of May, apparently, he had half made up his mind. He'd left no cairn at Cape Columbia, or any other point on the north shore of Ellesmere, recording his return from the pole. Now he decided to do so and sent Borup in charge of a sledge team with a note to be buried in a pile of rocks.

The cairn was opened in 1957 by Canadian Government employees stationed at Alert. Its message read:

"This monument marks the point of departure and return of the sledge expedition of the Peary Arctic Club, which in the spring of 1909 attained the North Pole. The members of the expedition taking part in the sledge work were Peary, Bartlett, Goodsell, Marvin, MacMillan, Borup and Henson."

Even this was still ambiguous. No date was given for attaining the pole, and the statement was not signed.

Also recovered from the cairn was an American flag, which was sent by mail to Peary's family.

In August the expedition worked its way southward to Anoatok, an

Inuit hunting station twenty-five miles north of Etah. Here they met the wealthy American hunter Harry Whitney, who had sailed north with them in 1908, and the really ugly things began to happen.

At Anoatok, the year before, Peary had confiscated a house, filled with supplies and furs, belonging to an explorer named Dr. Frederick Cook, a well-known veteran of the Arctic who had left on a journey toward the pole almost six months earlier. Regarding Cook as dead, and the supplies and furs as abandoned, Peary had taken charge of the entire cache and placed two of his men in the house, with orders to use the supplies in trade for more furs. He also confiscated the furs already there and sent them to market on his supply ship.

When Whitney met them, he announced that Cook was not dead after all. He had returned from a sledge journey of thirteen months (one of the longest ever undertaken successfully by a white man), reporting that he had reached the North Pole on April 21, 1908. Whitney had persuaded him to leave his diaries, papers, astronomical observations, and instruments with him for safekeeping, while Cook had continued by komatik down the west coast of Greenland, looking for a passage home.

Whitney asked for permission to bring Cook's materials on board the Roosevelt, but Peary refused to take them. He demanded from Whitney his "word as a gentleman" that he had not brought on board anything belonging to Dr. Cook. Whitney went to Matt Henson for advice, and Henson told him that the Commander was not to be trifled with in a matter of this kind.

So Whitney went ashore, with Bartlett for a witness, and buried Cook's records and instruments in a cache. They then returned to the Roosevelt and headed south.

On August 21 they steamed out of Smith Sound into the headwaters of Baffin Bay, and here, to their great surprise, they met a small schooner, the Jeanie, with Sam Bartlett, Bob's uncle, in command. She had been chartered by the Peary Arctic Club and sent north with a load of coal for the Roosevelt so that the fuel problems of her previous voyage would not be repeated.

The Jeanie brought news from Newfoundland and the world: the families of the explorers were all well. Four steel icebreakers, of a design new to the world, had been added to the Newfoundland sealing fleet that year. They were the *Florizel*, *Bellaventure*, *Bonaventure*, and *Beothic*. They had brought in bumper loads and opened a new era in ice navigation.

Sir Ernest Shackleton, leading a British expedition from New Zealand, had achieved a spectacular "furthest south," being forced to turn back a mere ninety-seven miles from the South Pole, and had been knighted for his achievement. Unlike the North Pole, which lay under a mile of water, the South Pole was on a plateau two miles high, and apparently in the middle of a continent.

At this point Harry Whitney, obviously uncomfortable on the *Roosevelt* with the Peary party, transferred to the *Jeanie* and went south with Sam Bartlett. Apparently Sam Bartlett offered to return for Dr. Cook's papers, and Whitney advised him not to go. He was trying his best to keep out of the storm of controversy that he saw brewing and to a large extent he was to succeed. His timidity—if that's what it was—did a grave disservice to the cause of historical truth. Cook's papers were never recovered.

The *Roosevelt* next called at Cape York, a harbor just north of Melville Bay, near the usual limit of open-water navigation. Here Peary found a letter addressed to him from Captain Adams of the Dundee whaler *Morning*, reporting that Adams had met Dr. Cook in southern Greenland in late June, that Cook had taken passage for Copenhagen, and that he claimed to have reached the North Pole on a sledge journey the year before.

Obviously, Cook was likely to beat Peary to the press wires. He gave orders that the *Roosevelt* was to sail immediately for Labrador. They called briefly at the Bartlett fishing station in Turnivik, then went on to Smokey where there was a telegraph station from which Peary sent his wire on September 5:

"Have made good at last. I have the pole."

Cook had beaten him by four days. He had wired from the Shetland Islands on September 1, and the American press had already hailed him in big black headlines as the conqueror of the pole.

Peary was furious. On September 8 he reached Battle Harbour, and from there he sent his famous wire:

"...Do not trouble about Cook's story....He has not been at the pole on April 21, 1908, or at any other time. He has simply handed the people a gold brick...."

Cook meanwhile, was in Copenhagen, attending massive celebrations in his honor. When he learned of Peary's charges, he hurried home to the United States to face a campaign of character assassination mounted by Peary and his supporters completely without precedent in the annals of exploration and almost unique until the time of Senator McCarthy and Richard Nixon.

Until then Cook had been a famous and honored explorer with a record at least as good as Peary's.

In 1891 he had served without pay as surgeon to Peary's expedition to north Greenland.

In 1893 he had made a three-month voyage in the Zeta along the shores of Baffin Bay and Smith Sound.

In 1894 he had made a hundred-mile arctic voyage in an open boat, seeking aid for the shipwrecked crew of the *Miranda*, which had been crushed in the ice. He was credited with saving them.

From 1897 to 1899 he served on the *Belgica*, the first ship to winter in the Antarctic. He was knighted by the king of Belgium for heroism during this expedition.

In 1901 he was sent north on the *Erik* to give aid to the Peary expedition that had set out for the pole in 1898 and had not been reported up to that time.

In 1903 he made an attempt to ascend Mount McKinley in Alaska, the highest peak in North America. He reported that he had failed.

In 1906 he made a second attempt on Mount McKinley, reported that he had succeeded, and published photographs taken from its summit. The Explorers' Club of New York honored Cook and Peary jointly as the two greatest American explorers of their time.

In 1907 he left for the pole, his modest expedition being financed by John R. Bradley, a millionaire American hunter who went north with Cook, provided him with logistic assistance, then reported back to the Explorers' Club that Cook was heading for the pole, and, if successful, would return in 1908. When he did not return that year, he was given up for lost.

Cook's story of his polar conquest, briefly summed up, was as follows:

He left Anoatok in northwest Greenland February 19, 1908, with one companion, Rudolph Francke, nine Inuit dog drivers, and eleven komatiks, carrying six thousand pounds of supplies. Advance parties had taken other supplies ahead to Ellesmere Island.

He crossed Ellesmere to Greely Fjord and Nansen Sound and went on to Svartevoeg, the cape at the northern tip of Axel Heiberg Island. (He was the third explorer to reach it, after Sverdrup and Peary.) At this point, five hundred and twenty miles from the pole, he took to the sea ice with two komatiks, twenty-six dogs, and thirteen hundred pounds of supplies, not counting gear, equipment, and ammunition. He and his two Inuit planned, if necessary, to eat twenty of the dogs and to return with only six. Francke and all but the two Inuit of the polar party then returned to Greenland. Cook left land March 19, 1908, reached the pole April 21, and started back. The outward trip had not been exceptionally difficult. The return trip was a nightmare. They ran into bad weather, loose ice, and fog, which prevented any celestial sights until June 13, when Cook finally obtained co-ordinates that placed him far to the westward of his intended route. He had missed Svartevoeg completely— it lay far off to the northeast—and he was heading for Ellef Ringnes Island.

Since it was now too late to get back to the food caches stored on Axel Heiberg Island, they continued south to Ellef Ringnes, then through Balcher Channel and Hell's Gate to Jones Sound. At Hell's Gate they abandoned their few remaining dogs and converted one of the sledges into a boat. (It had been designed for just that.) In this wood-and-canvas contraption they traveled a hundred miles through the waters of Jones Sound to Cape Sparbo, where they were forced to spend the winter in an old Inuit house, built partly underground by a people long since forgotten, near the foot of the immense Devon Island glacier.

Next spring they traveled eastward and northward, using a hand sledge, for three hundred miles to Cape Sabine, crossed the ice of Smith Sound, and were welcomed "back from the dead" by Inuit of Anoatok and by Harry Whitney, who was living there with them.

Even without the dash to the pole, this was perhaps the most remarkable sledge journey undertaken by any white man up to that time. It sounded impossible, like something straight out of a boy's adventure story, and Peary had fun tearing it to pieces. He "proved" by clever arguments that Cook could never have been in the interior of Ellesmere Island, that he had never been on Axel Heiberg Island, and that his claim to have journeyed over the polar ice was impossible.

He and his supporters went back to Cook's Mount McKinley climb and tried to prove he had never done it. They mounted a savage newspaper campaign describing him everywhere as a fraud. They falsified his own statements to make it appear that he had contradicted himself and that he admitted he might not, after all, have reached the pole. He was finally hounded into prison on a completely false charge of stock fraud involving a sale of oil properties that later yielded their owners millions of tons of crude oil, though Cook had sold them for a song. Even after he was proven innocent, he was left in jail for years, until the American Government was shamed into releasing him in 1930. A generation after the charge of fraud was totally disproven, it is still brought against Cook by Peary supporters.

All this for daring to claim that he had reached the pole first. Had the year been 1909 instead of 1908, none of it would have happened.

It must be said to Bartlett's credit that he took very little part in this campaign of slander. He later established that Cook had indeed been in Jones Sound, as he said, and had wintered at an abandoned Inuit house on Devon Island, and he revealed these facts to the world, even though they did nothing for his own or Peary's reputations.

Like Peary, Cook could not prove that he had been at the pole. His story had to stand, in the end, on the circumstantial detail that it contained. Fortunately for Cook's eventual reputation, there was a great deal of this circumstantial detail, and, except in one point, it was later confirmed by other explorers. The false detail was his report of "Bradley Land," off to the northwest of Axel Heiberg Island, glimpsed along the horizon from a great distance. Like Peary's Crocker Land, which it strongly resembled, it simply isn't there.

Effie M. Morrissey moored to a huge ice pan during one of the East Greenland expeditions.

Bartlett's crew using saws to cut a lane through an ice floe off the coast of Greenland.

Captain Bartlett on top of the Peary memorial that he erected at
Cape York, northwest Greenland.

Trapped in heavy ice, the *Morrissey* is almost buried, but in
twenty expeditions she was never badly damaged.

Morrissey at Turnivik, the Bartlett fishing station on a desolate island off the coast of Labrador.

Bob's nephew, Rupert, now Judge Bartlett of Brigus, sorting and preserving specimens for the Smithsonian Institution.

Polar bear cub, in harness on deck, heading for a zoo. Bartlett also lassoed the first adult male polar bear, the famous Silver King that lived for twenty years in captivity.

Inuk ivory carver at Iglulik. Traditional carving is all in ivory. Until recently soapstone was used only for pots.

"Raftered" ice between Shipwreck Camp and Wrangel Island. Only Bartlett's determination got men, dogs, and sledges through the likes of this.

Shipwreck Camp, Arctic Ocean, after the *Karluk* sank, February 1914. "Without Captain Bartlett we would all have died right there," Ernest Chafe reported.

Panorama of Brigus in Captain Bartlett's time. The "pond" at the inner end of the harbor is shown.

One of the most beautiful bergs on record, photographed by Bartlett in Baffin Bay. About a third of a mile long, it rose some four hundred feet above the water.

The Arctic is often peaceful, almost idyllic. It was the only place where Bartlett was happy.

Family of walrus in loose ice. Some of Bartlett's expeditions were made specifically to capture arctic animals.

Bartlett's bumper voyage as a sealing captain was made in the famous *Neptune*, here loading pelts in a solid icc jam. "Far more dangerous than arctic exploration," he said.

The *Beothic* in 1910, "coming home on her tank tops" after Bartlett took her to Ellesmere Island and into Jones and Lancaster sounds.

Three crewmen attempting to pry heavy ice floes apart to make way for the ship.

A dog team leaving the *Morrissey* to take explorers to the coast of Greenland.

The circumstantial detail provided by Cook included a major correction to the map of Axel Heiberg Island as drawn by Sverdrup. A piece of land that Sverdrup reported as an island, Cook correctly recognized as a peninsula. So Cook had been on Axel Heiberg Island after all. To get there he must have crossed Ellesmere, as he claimed.

Peary supporters next confined themselves to "proving" that Cook could never have gotten out of sight of land on the Arctic Ocean and even concocted a story said to have been told by his two Inuit companions to this effect. But here, again, he has been justified by time.

He reported an open lead at the edge of the continental shelf north of Axel Heiberg Island in exactly the place where later surveys proved it to be. The ice conditions that he described for his polar journey were precisely the conditions that have since been found to prevail in the central arctic basin. He was the first to report the clockwise drift of ice between Axel Heiberg and the pole and the rending and breaking of ice pans along the course of the westerly current.

But the thing that clinches the matter was his discovery of the ice islands: "With our dogs bounding and tearing onward, from the eighty-seventh to the eighty-eighth parallel we passed for two days over old ice without pressure lines or hummocks. There was no discernible line of demarcation to indicate separate fields, and it was quite impossible to determine whether we were on land or sea ice. The barometer indicated no perceptible elevation, but the ice had the hard, wavering surface of glacial ice, with only superficial crevasses. The water obtained from this was not salty."

This description tallies exactly with the floating ice islands that were not officially known to the world until after the Second World War. They looked like glacial ice because they *are* glacial ice. They are vast, flat icebergs calved from the glacial ice shelf of Ellesmere Island. But their nature and origin were not known until the 1950s. Up to that time Cook had been the only person to report them.

There is no way Cook could have invented or imagined these vast fields of glacial ice with a wavy surface within two-hundred miles of the pole without having been there to see it. The position he gave for his two ice islands coincides exactly with the drift tracks measured in the 1950s.

J. Fletcher, leader of the American team on ice island T-3, was quoted as saying: "It is impossible to believe that Cook lied. It would not have been possible for him to have fabricated such a story on the basis of the then available knowledge of ice conditions and drift in the arctic basin."

There is no way Cook could have invented the position of the continental slope either, or guessed there was a westerly flowing current beyond the edge of the shelf. It is now practically certain that he found the ice islands just where he said he did—approximately a hundred and fifty to two hundred miles from the pole.

There are other details concerning the thickness and the nature of the ice, temperatures, drift, and so on, in all of which Cook's story agrees with present-day discoveries, and places it beyond doubt that he must have made a long journey over the Arctic Ocean. The question was analyzed by a Soviet scientist, V. S. Koryakin of the Academy of Sciences of the U.S.S.R., in a lengthy paper published in 1975. His conclusion was that Cook bad gone exactly where he said he did.

But the monstrous injustice done to Cook by Peary, MacMillan, Borup, and the Peary supporters in the United States has never been righted. He died neglected and disgraced, his legitimate discoveries discredited, and it seems likely that the situation will remain that way in his own country. Only in Europe, and, more recently, in Canada, is it coming to be realized that his claim to the pole is at least as good as Peary's, and the story of his sledge journey a lot more plausible. (His supplies were sufficient to last the time he said they did. His speeds were reasonable. His best time over the sea ice was only 21 miles a day, compared with Peary's 75½. But neither Cook nor Peary was ever able to offer proof that he had actually been at 90° N.

The whole business was utterly sordid and belittled the real achievement, as Bartlett found to his cost. He was honored by such American groups as the Explorers' Club and the National Geographic Society. He was received by the king of Italy and other European nobility. He made a lot of money, by the standards of the time, on the lecture circuit. Then, quickly, he began to sink into obscurity. Only in Newfoundland, where he was a national hero, did his name really live. When Canadians began reviving their own history in the 1960s and writing accounts of the exploration of the country, the name of their greatest explorer of all, Robert Bartlett, had been forgotten.

Even more remarkable, perhaps, is his omission from *The National Atlas of Canada*, published in 1974, with an eight-page section devoted to exploration, and maps purporting to give the routes of all the important voyages in the Canadian north. It is scarcely credible that the compilers of the atlas were ignorant of the existence of the man who had received the Hubbard Medal for exploration in the Canadian Arctic, and who had made more voyages into Canadian arctic waters than anyone before or since, but it seems they must have been.

Bartlett and Peary remained on friendly terms until Peary's death but were never again associated in any public way. Peary, in fact, dropped rapidly out of the public eye after the first months of furious controversy and after the row with Cook appeared to be settled in his favor. Except for a few ceremonial appearances, he remained in retirement from 1910 until he died in 1920, lying on a musk-ox skin, gazing out toward the waters of Chesapeake Bay.

9

"Hunting...if you can call it that."

Nineteen hundred and ten was Bartlett's big year. For a brief time he knew the taste of glory. He went on a lecture tour of Europe, speaking to world-renowned societies and scientific bodies, meeting scientists, business magnates, and aristocrats in a world where all those things still counted.

The First World War, which ended the nineteenth century and ushered in the twentieth, was four years away, and Europe still glittered. It was a world with a thirst for heroes, on the brink of its own death, but thrilling to vicarious adventures, a world that had created Livingston and General Gordon and Florence Nightingale and, two years later, would make a kind of dying god out of "Scott of the Antarctic."

Meanwhile, it had men like Bartlett ready and eager to thrill its decadent soul with accounts of deeds larger than life, carried out with inflexible will amid dangers more terrible than death. He was always a great success as a lecturer, articulate, self-confident, full of his subject, and—at a time when "coarse language" was supposed to be totally taboo—his accounts were always well salted with vulgarities and profanities that made dowagers and duchesses blush deliciously behind their fans.

While still in Europe, he received a request to be captain of another expedition into the Arctic and promptly cut his tour short. This time they would not be going in search of undiscovered places and would have to make no pretense of collecting scientific information; it was simply to be a shooting spree. Harry Whitney and another millionaire playboy named Paul Rainey were ready to spend a hundred thousand dollars to see how many musk ox, walrus, and polar bears they could slaughter in a single season.

Whitney, of course, had spent summers and even winters in north Greenland, but this time he was planning something different. He wanted to go right up among the islands of the Northwest Passage, where no sportsman had ever been before, and he wanted to do it in style.

Nothing easier. Bartlett returned from Europe on the luxury liner *Mauritania*, and at Boston joined the *Beothic*, one of the new steel icebreakers that had proved such a success at the Newfoundland seal hunt the year before. These icebreakers, designed to crush heavy ice with their weight, rather than by backing off and butting at it, were the first ships ever designed specifically to navigate (not drift) in arctic ice fields.

The hunters paid $70,000 to charter and outfit the ship. Then they sailed for Greenland, Baffinland, and points north and west.

Bartlett gave them their money's worth. He took them to Greenland and Baffinland and into Lancaster Sound and Jones Sound, to the shores of Devon Island and Ellesmere Island, on voyages that had stopped many a famous explorer. But no famous explorer before Bartlett's time had ever had a ship like the *Beothic*, a compact steel icebreaker, 471 tons net, with a reinforced hull, round bows, shallower forward than aft, coal-burning engines that would drive her at fourteen knots, so strongly constructed that she could back off and ram an ice floe at full power. When compared with the *Beothic*, the *Roosevelt* was already totally obsolete.

This was the first of a series of "scenic" voyages that Bartlett made to the eastern Arctic and seems to have been the one on which he realized the potential of the camera. From that time forward, he always carried an official photographer, and, in total, he produced a stunning array of photographs and film reels from the most spectacular region of eastern North America.

Their first stop was Melville Bay in northwestern Greenland, an area Bartlett now knew by heart. It is the birthplace of most of the world's icebergs, for here the mile-thick Greenland ice cap touches the sea and splits into great floating chunks, some of them three or four square miles in area, many as large as a ball park, and a few as tall as the CN tower in Toronto. Looking at one of these monsters, it's hard to believe that nine tenths of its bulk lies under water, but you'd better remember it, if you don't want to be wrecked.

"There is a savage grandeur in this coast," Bartlett wrote "for it is carved by the eternal conflict with storms and glaciers, bergs and grinding ice fields. But behind the frowning outer mass nestles many grass-carpeted, flower-sprinkled, sun-kissed nooks… poppies, dandelions, buttercups, saxifrage… millions of little auks breed along this shore… glaciers launch their fleets of bergs… masses of glistening ice of all shapes and sizes."

On this trip they called at North Star Bay. There were no houses there, just a few tents, and in one of the tents Bartlett visited a man who was lying ill — his first meeting with Knud Rasmussen, whose mother was Inuit and whose father was Danish. This man was later to change the name of North Star Bay to Thule and make it world-famous. (When Bartlett visited the same spot twenty-five years later, Rasmussen was dead, but Thule was the most important place in the High Arctic.)

On August 4, they reached Anoatok and opened the cairn where Whitney had buried Cook's materials the year before. They found that the cairn had already been opened and the papers that Whitney had buried were gone. At least that was their story. While at Anoatok they were joined by another party, including John R. Bradley, the backer of the Cook expedition, also looking for Cook's records.

Bartlett subsequently felt compelled to defend himself against the charge that he had destroyed or lost Cook's records.

"Of his belongings there remained a few clothes and such like, and certainly a sextant," Bartlett affirmed. "As for records, I will stake my life on it, there were none there."

It is unfortunate that Bradley was not present when the cairn was first opened. Had he been, the partisans of Cook would not have been able to accuse Bartlett, as they later did, of the unauthorized removal of Cook's records.

At Anoatok they hired Inuit guides and hunters and turned west toward the almost-virgin islands of the Canadian Arctic Archipelago. Here, on August 15, 1910, they captured Silver King, a six-year-old male polar bear, the first full-grown male ever taken alive.

Bartlett's account of this adventure in the mouth of Jones Sound is as follows:

"It was midnight, not a cloud in the sky, not a breath of wind, and the smoke of the funnel going straight up. I was in the crow's-nest, and moving my glasses along the rim of the barrel I saw the bear stalking a seal. For a little while I watched him, and then I moved the ship towards him, but he did not see, smell or hear us until I was right on top of him.

"I headed the bow of the ship in such a way that I pried off the point of ice that he was on, and as the vessel kept going ahead she shoved the bear and the ice into the open water. I maneuvered the *Beothic* so that I kept him away from the land ice, as once he regained that we could never catch him. We didn't want him dead but alive for Dr. Hornaday of the Bronx Zoo.

"On board we had two big launches built by Lawley of S. Boston, and in each one a 45 horsepower standard gasoline engine. This was lowered, and in it went Daugler, Paul's chauffeur, one of the sailors, Paul and myself. I put the sailor to the tiller, Daugler to the engine, and I went forward with the rope. By this time we had the bear well out clear of the island, and I told the Mate to keep the ship between it and the land ice. If he went in the direction of the land ice, to head him off.

"I then threw the noose over his head and, being in a hurry, tightened it up, which wasn't so good, for it jammed his wind, so I worked it off him by slackening up the rope and keeping up close to him in the launch, then shoving it over his foreshoulders with the long boat hook. Now the fun began. He towed us, and in spite of the fact that we went astern on the engine, he could still tow us. I signalled the ship to come up, and we drew in alongside, abreast of No. 1 hold, which was empty of coal. I had them lower the steel fall, and with a double wall knot in the manilla lariat we began to hoist him up, but before the slack was taken up he got it in his teeth and chewed it off.

"We followed him, and I picked up the end of the rope, holding him until the ship came up again. This time we held the rope tight until the strain came on the fall, but while we were doing this he tried to get aboard our launch, and you should have seen the splinters fly from the gun-whales as he tackled them with his teeth.... As he went over the rail, he made one mighty effort to get clear, but once clear of the rail, we lowered him right into No. 1 hold where we kept him until we built a large cage of planks.

"We lowered it into the hold, but like a sensible bear he would not (go) inside, so I suggested to Paul that he go down and drive him in, but like myself he didn't relish that job. We then hoisted the cage on deck, put a trap door in the top with a sliding door of iron bars and lowered a bucket of water through it. Immediately he went in, and once inside we had him secure.

"All the time we were up north we had no trouble with him, but when we came south we took him on deck so we could give him a good wash with the hose. At Battle Harbour, Labrador, we found a radio message asking us to dinner at Mrs. Joe Harriman's, Newport, R.I. We accepted, or at least Paul did, for us all, and we made it, but the night before going ashore the bear almost got away from us. It was one of those close, rainy nights, dark as a grave, but fortunately we saw him make the attempt, and a crowd of us were near enough to push him back with capstan bars. Had he gotten out, he would have been overboard into the harbor, and ashore, and believe me before he was subdued, he would have raised merry hell in and around the Casino. We landed him at the dock at City Island. Dr. Ditmars from the Zoo came down with a big covered-in truck, and as I remember he gave him about eighteen pounds of chloroform. When we landed him he weighed 1,200 pounds, and lived until 1931."

After capturing this animal, Bartlett steamed through Lady Ann Strait into Jones Sound, where three of the world's greatest glaciers, remnants of a vast ice sheet that once covered the entire region, rise to heights of more than a mile on either hand. While in Jones Sound they visited Cape Sparbo, went ashore, and confirmed Cook's report that he had spent the winter in the ruins of an ancient Inuit house, half cave, with what had once been a roof made of stones and bones, now fallen in.

They worked their way south into Lancaster Sound, the true Northwest Passage, and met great fields of ice running eastward into Baffin Bay. Here the *Boothia* took her greatest battering of the year and came close to being sunk by ice sheets closing in from both sides, but Bartlett's usual luck held and they escaped with merely a few holes in her double bottom.

The hunting everywhere was all that the most bloodthirsty sportsman could have wished. They killed fifty-nine polar bears that summer—probably an all—time record for a single hunting party. They brought home three live bears—two young ones in addition to Silver King—two baby walrus, and six baby musk ox to be sold to zoos. They didn't count the walrus and musk ox they slaughtered. Though Bartlett mentioned two herds, with a total of twenty-four animals killed or captured on Devon Island, presumably this was only one of several successful musk-ox hunts. He insisted that none of the meat was wasted but was landed in Greenland to feed men and dogs.

This kind of "sport" seems barbarous, and even shocking, today, when musk ox and polar bears have been reduced to near extinction, and when the occasional hunter who still goes after big game is content to kill a single animal, or perhaps try for a "trophy head" if it's the kind of thing you mount. But in 1910 it was quite normal. Sportsmen, in those days, were still frankly and honestly out for blood, and killing your first bear only whetted your appetite for the next. On this kind of hunt, Bartlett reported, you carried 100,000 rounds of ammunition and shot at everything that swam, walked, or flew. He mentioned it with contempt as "hunting, if you can call it that," but he was quite willing to be employed by now, he had developed a great yearning. From the age of twenty-three until his death at the age of seventy, he never spent a summer anywhere else if he could help it.

The expedition certainly helped to deplete, and probably did permanent damage to, the herds of animals in a part of the Arctic over which Canada had just then asserted sovereignty. It was also nearly fatal to the ship. Once west of Baffin Bay, they were into uncharted waters, where reefs and banks were complicated by running ice in which even the *Beothic* was sometimes unable to choose her own course. They touched bottom an uncounted number of times—Bartlett literally didn't bother to note all the minor groundings in his log—and ran solidly on the rocks on five different occasions.

As usual he came to no serious harm. He always seemed to be able to take chances that would have been fatal to anyone else but that to him were merely a lark. Every time they ran hard aground they either got off with the tide or by the use of their winches—not one of the many strandings disabled the ship.

The *Beothic*, in Bartlett's phrase, "came home on her tank tops," by which he meant that her bottom was gone and she was floating on the waterproof tanks that lined her holds.

When they put her on dock, they found her plates punctured from stem to stern, and the repair bill came to $25,000 (a quarter of a million, at least, in today's funds). It was paid cheerfully by Whitney and Rainey. They'd never had such fun in their lives and were already planning to go again another year.

Bartlett was not simply captain of the ship that took Rainey and Whitney on this voyage, but a close personal friend of the two millionaires as well. He had known Whitney for a long time. Rainey he had first met the year before when he was being lionized at a dinner in New York.

On their return from the massive hunt, Bartlett and Rainey went out on the town together. Rainey, at least, did a lot of drinking that evening and tried his luck against the house in one or more gambling dens. Bartlett followed him to a club "up in the Fifties" in New York City and He called Bartlett aside, said, "Here, I want you to hold this for me," and passed over a wad of bills.

"I didn't look at the money," Bartlett said, "but jammed it down into my jeans, only too glad to help." They spent the rest of the evening whooping it up in the city's hot spots, then took cabs to their separate hotels. "I got home about three o'clock in the morning after a not altogether unamusing evening," Bartlett recalled. "While I was undressing I suddenly remembered the money.... Imagine my horror when I discovered he had given me sixteen thousand-dollar bills. I'd never seen so much money in my life. I was scared stiff. I locked the door and put the washstand against it....

"That afternoon I met him at the club."

At the Explorers' Club, Rainey, still looking a little shakey, asked Bartlett if he hadn't passed something over to him the night before. Bartlett, thinking to frighten him, at first pretended to be puzzled. Then, realizing that Rainey was only mildly interested in the question of whether or not he had lost sixteen thousand dollars at gambling, he laughed and pulled out the roll.

Rainey didn't even bother to count it. He peeled off two one-thousand-bills, passed them over to his friend, and stuffed the rest in his pocket. The two thousand dollars was payment for Bartlett's summer in the Arctic. It was typical of him that he had made no arrangement about payment in advance. For most of his voyages he never collected a cent in wages.

10

"I got to be a mangy lion..."

Every spring that he wasn't locked away in the Arctic, Bob Bartlett went sealing. He made a number of successful trips with his father or with one of his uncles and helped to bring in bumper loads as mate or second hand, as the sealing mate was called. But as master of sealing ships he was a conspicuous failure. He tried many times, even getting command of one of the new icebreakers, owned by Bowrings. Who would deny a simple thing like command of a sealing ship to a captain as famous as Bartlett? But usually something happened to ruin the voyage. His brother Will says he was too impatient to make a successful sealing captain. Whatever the cause, he came back with "bad trips."

His failure as a sealer was one of the causes of the deepening depression that seized him in the years after the North Pole voyages.

There were other causes, too; the greatest, perhaps, being the aftermath of the *Karluk* expedition. He returned to Newfoundland in 1914, after the sinking of the *Karluk*, a national hero. But then he had to face an admiralty commission that found him at fault for ever putting the *Karluk* into the ice against his better judgment. He was also found at fault for allowing the "doctor's party" to set out for shore, even though its members had signed a paper absolving him from all responsibility in their rash attempt to do it on their own. The commission's findings were clearly unfair and ran counter to both public and professional opinion, but still they rankled.

Stefansson, as well as Bartlett, suffered public attack as a result of the *Karluk* sinking. When he was being considered for the presidency of the Explorers' Club in New York, Dr. Anderson, the leader of the southern group that had split off from the expedition and declared its independence from Stefansson, denounced him to the club as a socialist, a pacifist, and a coward and accused him of abandoning the *Karluk* and her crew when he knew she was in danger.

All this, it has been suggested, was the reason Bartlett decided, late in life, to take out American citizenship and to settle permanently in New York. But his brother Will, who sailed as mate on all his later voyages and who knew him as well as anybody, says the main reason was that nobody except Americans would back his arctic expeditions, and they objected to giving their backing to a foreigner. He was still living in Peary's shadow and dealing with the same group that had financed Peary.

During the First World War, Bartlett worked for the American Army Transport Command, ferrying troops and supplies. He hated the work. Most of the time he was ashore or on short voyages between American mainland ports. He made one voyage to Honolulu with a load of dynamite. ("When we passed through the Panama Canal they treated us like we had leprosy.") But even this failed to interest him. He was restless and discontented and felt that he should have been overseas fighting the Germans, where two of his younger brothers were killed, one by enemy fire in Europe, one by anthrax in the Near East.

For a brief time he became Lieutenant Commander Bartlett, U.S.N.,

having been transferred from the army to the navy so he could go to
rescue an American naval ship that was frozen into the ice of the St.
Lawrence. This created a flicker of interest, and he wished he had time
for a visit to Brigus to show off his blue uniform and gold stripes, but the
job of rescuing the ship proved childishly simple, completely without
challenge. He spent most of the war period in a fretting fury over the
bungling American bureaucracy with which he was involved.

In 1917 he had a chance, for the first time in three years, to make some
real use of his talents as an ice skipper.

In 1913 Donald B. MacMillan, one of Peary's bright young men, had
been put in charge of an expedition to discover and explore Crocker
Land, the island, or perhaps continent, supposed to lie northwest of
Ellesmere, sighted and named by Peary, in 1906.

The Crocker Land Expedition was the last great American effort in
the High Arctic before aircraft took over the job of exploration. Besides
planting the Stars and Stripes on a new land, the expedition had another
motive: to prove once and for all that Dr. Frederick Cook was a liar and
a fraud. Crocker Land, according to Peary, lay right smack-dab in the
middle of the route by which Dr. Cook claimed to have sledged
homeward from the pole, meeting nothing but ice all the way. When
MacMillan had fixed the exact position of Crocker Land, Dr. Cook
would be disposed of, once and for all.

The Crocker Land Expedition, like Cook before it, found nothing but
ocean northwest of Ellesmere, but on returning to Smith Sound, they
found that relief ships had been unable to get into Etah, their home base.
This didn't worry MacMillan. By now he had discovered that you could
live indefinitely on the hunting expertise of the Inuit, and he was quite
prepared to spend three years or ten years in the Arctic—there was no
danger that his men would starve and resort to cannibalism, like those
under the command of the incompetent Greely, thirty-five years earlier.
But memories of the Greely disaster, the worst of it still only told in
whispers, were strong in the minds of his American backers. After three
relief ships had failed to get through the ice to Etah, they finally
commissioned Bob Bartlett to go to MacMillan's rescue in the ancient
Newfoundland sealer *Neptune*, a veteran of polar ice at both ends of the

earth.

Even Bartlett had some difficulty with the Baffin Bay ice pack that summer. It took him twelve days to work his way across the two hundred miles of Melville Bay. Then he found the *Danmark*, the last supply ship sent in search of MacMillan, frozen in at Cape Parry, just south of Smith Sound. He took off the *Danmark*'s supplies and headed for Etah, arriving July 1, 1917, with a canvas patch covering a hole that he had punched in the *Neptune*'s bow while butting through ice. He noted in his log, with pardonable pride, that this was the third major American arctic expedition that had been rescued by a Bartlett from Brigus.

Back in New York, the war over, he began a determined campaign to launch a major exploring effort into the arctic basin. This was not to be a mere dash to the pole, or a mere search for some chunk of land previously unvisited by man, but a true scientific expedition to map the world's only unknown ocean, discover the nature of its continental slopes and deeps, and establish the pattern of its winds and currents.

He wanted to build a diesel-powered, steel-reinforced ship that could be put into the ice in the north and west in a position from which, as the drifts of the *Fram* and the *Jeannette* indicated, it should be carried in the ice right across the pole and on across the Arctic to the east coast of Greenland.

The ship was a new design of his own, based on both his knowledge of the *Roosevelt* and his experience with Newfoundland icebreakers. He was convinced that he could build a much abler ship than the *Fram*, more capable of moving under her own power among the northern ice fields, but one that it would still be impossible for the polar pack to crush.

He got private backing totaling $100,000 for this project, but it was not enough. He failed to get backing from the American Government, as he had hoped. He received a tender from a shipyard for the building of this radical exploring ship, and it was disappointingly high—$210,500. It looked as if he'd need half a million, all told, and there seemed to be no way to get it without the backing of the American Navy. High-ranking naval men agreed and sought government approval, but they failed, finally, to get the agreement of the President.

Bartlett pursued this project for years. Finally, the "Bartlett Arctic

Council" was formed to carry out the plan. It included men from the scientific branches of the American Government, the Carnegie Institution, various universities and scientific societies, and the British Admiralty. A place was held open for a representative of the Canadian Naval Service, but it was never filled. After the complete bungling mess they had made of the *Karluk* expedition, the Canadian Government was having nothing more to do with the Arctic. The Americans could have it, and welcome (and they almost did).

Meanwhile, the American Navy had decided that the greatest publicity value in polar exploration in the future would be in spectacular flying stunts—and publicity was what everybody wanted, not just for the glory of it, either, but because that was the way you got the big appropriations of money.

Bartlett pointed out that there could be few if any scientific results from a mere endurance flight in a plane or airship over the arctic basin. Planes had no equipment to measure depths or currents or to collect any kind of data from the surface. He was right. (When Richard E. Byrd [a close friend of his] and Umberto Nobile and Roald Amundsen finally did it, in 1926, both in the same week, one in an airplane, the other in an airship, the scientific results were zero.)

Here is one of his proposals, dated 1924:

Memorandum of an Arctic Drift Project

Nothing in this world has interested me more than the fauna and flora of the Arctic seas. This is partly just a natural interest and partly it is the result of experience over a good many years in Arctic regions where one is always at the door of the unknown. Fully two million square miles of unknown territory remains unexplored. Until scientific investigation has penetrated this great region we shall not know accurately the contour of the floor of the polar basin nor the form and position of the continental shelf about the basin border. To explore the extent, depth and character of the polar basin is to my mind one of the very greatest tasks yet awaiting investigation.

It is only in recent years that little or any notice has been paid to Oceanography. In this country, Agassiz of Harvard, Admirals Chester Pillsbury, Sigsbee, and Admiral Bartlett and President Jordan were pioneers. On the other side of the water we have the Norwegians, the English, and the Prince of Monaco, the Norwegians leading in scientific research as well as in commerce.

Here is an opportunity for me to do something worthwhile and make a howling success of it. Physically I am as fit as ever I was, and mentally far ahead of what I was when with Peary. Today I am more experienced and know how to handle the situation, and how to go after the things that will spell success to the expedition. DeLong's drift in the *Jeannette* and the *Fram's* drift have shown a little of what might be expected from the up-to-date equipped ship were she to go into the polar basin.

In addition to the physical features of the ocean floor it is necessary to measure the currents of the Arctic as to width, direction, velocity, volume. There is also the question of the salinity of the water at the surface and down toward the bottom at various depths. It may be possible to anchor in the big leads of the water and take a round of tidal observation. With the current gauges brought up to date one should have no difficulty in getting very accurate measurements of the speed and volume of the currents. There is really a great deal to learn about the currents in the polar basin as to direction, force and volume; and also as to whether we have the same fall and change as in the Gulf Stream or whether it is a current similar only in a small degree to that stream. Knowledge of the northernmost limit of the Japan Current is also lacking, and a study of the plankton and diatoms brought northward on its surface would command my special attention.

Since international co-operation was begun through a series of internationally maintained arctic stations at the

time of Greely's expeditions in the late 80s it is surprising
how little has been learned about the wind system of the
Arctic and its effect upon the currents of the sea. It would
be one of my purposes to extend our knowledge of arctic
meteorology by taking observations upon the wind velocity
from day to day not merely over a period of weeks and
months but for the several years that I intend to stay there.
In connection with the meteorology I should plan to study
the effect of the wind, both the occasional wind and the
more regular wind, upon currents and ice movement.

Peary and I often went over the possibilities of the drift as
I am here anticipating it. I was so sorry that our sounding
wire was broken so often and leads lost. This eventually left
us only a bare 1,500 fathoms of wire, and at the pole the
sounding showed no bottom at 1,500 fathoms. I should plan
to explore with captive balloons the state of the air several
thousand feet above the ice, determining its temperature,
pressure, and its movements both in time of storm and in
relative calm. This would be useful to weather bureaus all
over the world. With our high power wireless we can give
out a report of the weather in general and of the storms
where we are, from time to time broadcasting their starting
point, intensity, etc. A report of the path of the storm
through North American areas or Europe might reach the
farmer and the mariner in time to warn him. The information would surely be of inestimable value and interest,
suppose we are three years drifting. All this data compiled
can be taken as a guide for future reference.

All of the Oceanography done in the North Atlantic and
the Pacific must be linked up with the work in the Arctic
Ocean, and the distribution and migratory habits of fish like
the cod, herring and halibut, as well as the whale. An
airplane could be carried along to do scout work during the
fine warm days in June and July as it is no trouble nowadays
to use aeroplanes or boats for distances of say 500 miles from

the ship. For instance, if new land is sighted the aeroplane will be sent to photograph and take measurements, instead of sending sledges and dogs. The ship could always be picked up by the aid of a smoke screen. One thing is certain—that no relief expedition is to be thought of. We can always return in the event of losing our ship, but with a new ship, built and strengthened as my ship will be, once away from land the danger of losing her is very remote.

Drifting in the ice, we can procure specimens in the dredger to depths of 2,500 fathoms, for the reason that conditions are so much better than on shipboard, especially in weather where the ship is rolling and tumbling about. On the floe you have smooth water and plenty of room to work. At the stern of the ship and on the floe we shall always leave a large hole made through the ice, and over this a snow-house strengthened by wood rafters and canvas walls and roof, and a gasoline engine to generate our light and to lift our wire attached to our dredger. When the dredger comes to the surface its contents will be removed and classified right away, and put in glass jars on the shelves of the laboratory. This, by the way, will be built on the design of one who knows just how such a place should be built, and equipped with up-to-date materials. We shall have a place to develop our moving picture film so that we can see from time to time what luck we are having with our pictures. There are many things which I have left out that we shall do. We shall take every care to have a good type of scientist and one who loves his work. I am going at this because I love to do it and want to make it a success.

It will take $150,000. I already have the engine, windlass and winch, costing some $30,000; also cameras and instruments. The ship, which will be built of wood, will be about 125 feet long and 36 feet abeam. The plans and specifications have been approved and passed before the American Bureau of Shipping. The ship will be built on the west coast

of the United States of America. It will take six months to
build and equip her. Ten men will accompany me. The
scientists will be one magnetician, one marine biologist, and
one map maker. The balance will be from Newfoundland,
consisting of sealers and fishermen, wireless operators and
flyers. We shall have fifty dogs and the provisions will be of
the best. I expect to do this drift in three years although I
shall provision for five. I will not put the ship in the ice until
late in the fall. It will be anywhere between Drift Cask No.
26 and Point Barrow. I expect to cross the polar sea in very
high latitudes and come out three years later in the Atlantic.
We shall have a cold storage plant on board where we can
store fresh reindeer meat which we can get in Alaska. We
shall also get all the seals, bears and walrus possible so as to
make the stock of fresh meat adequate. Col. E. Lester Jones
of the U. S. Coast and Geodetic Survey will furnish me with
the instruments and men I need, and Dr. Bauer of the
Department of Terrestrial Magnetism, Carnegie Institution
of Washington, will give me all the help possible.

I have quoted this proposal at length to show Bartlett's interests and
the extent to which he was ahead of his time. All the things he proposed
were eventually done—mainly by the Russians. Not until 1937, when
they landed a massive expedition by four-engined aircraft at the pole—
one section of which set out to drift from there to the east coast of
Greenland, where it was picked up by a Soviet icebreaker, bringing back
with it an incredible wealth of new information—was any really detailed
knowledge of the Arctic Ocean available to science. They continued
their work after the Second World War by aircraft and icebreaker and
by drifts on ice islands, mapping the floor of the Arctic, discovering its
mid-ocean ridge, the nature of its currents and winds, and cataloguing
its life—all the work that Bartlett had laid out for himself, but was unable
to get the backing to do, in the years immediately following the First
World War.

Disappointed in this, and in all his proposals for arctic exploration,

Bartlett slid rapidly to the lowest point of his life.

He never admitted, publicly, that he was a drinker. The nearest he came to it was in his book, *The Log*, in which he confessed that he fell into "a spell of drifting in the years after the war." From being a social lion, he said, "I got to be a mangy lion... a has-been who was being carted around to a free dinner here and there in hopes that he would break out into some rich sea tale and stage a freak monologue free of charge."

He didn't mention alcohol. Reading his published papers, you are led to believe that he was a teetotaler all his life. Nothing could be further from the truth. Perhaps he wanted to hide it to spare his mother's feelings, and those of other members of his family in Brigus. Whatever the reason, he was desperately ashamed of the years when he was just a short step from New York's Skid Row, and because of this he was never able to claim credit for the great victory that he eventually won over himself.

In the ten years following the *Karluk* expedition, Bartlett discovered the meaning of despair, and explored all the corners of the black night of the soul. He drank only moderately during the war, but was often depressed. When the war ended, his depression increased, and his drinking increased with it. Soon he had gained such a reputation as an incurable drunk that he had trouble getting any backing for a voyage— even a voyage by sportsmen like Whitney and Rainey, much less the ambitious arctic drift on which his heart was set.

An exception was the *National Geographic*. They remained friendly, and sent him to Alaska in 1923 as a passenger on the *Bear*, the patrol ship that had once been a sealer and, like the *Neptune*, made voyages into the ice at both ends of the earth. Bartlett did not get along well with the ship's captain, did almost no work during the voyage, and produced little that the *National Geographic* could publish. He returned in a state of black depression to another year of solitary drinking in his New York hotel room, a routine that he varied, whenever he got the chance, by social drinking with his millionaire friends.

Prohibition was law at the time, but that made no difference. Bartlett had a standing order with a New York bootlegger for a regular supply of black-market whiskey. He had become a character, old "Cap'n Bob," head softened by liquor, always good for an off-color yarn at a stag party, provided you gave him a free meal.

One day he woke up in the middle of a millionaires' dinner (eight cocktails having gone down before it started) and realized they were laughing at him, waiting for him to perform. Sullenly he refused and decided he was going to stop this kind of life. But stopping wasn't easy. He was eating at free lunches in clubs and paying his hotel bill from handouts.

Then, in the winter of 1924, the man who had survived six voyages into the arctic ice without injury, and had walked ashore from three total wrecks, was almost killed on the street by a laundry wagon. Hit while crossing New York's Forty-fourth Street, he suffered a broken leg and several broken ribs. The leg gave him so much trouble that he spent three months in the hospital.

Afterward he walked with a limp, but not for long. He regained excellent health, took off most of the surplus weight he had accumulated in his sodden years on the beach (though to the end of his life he continued to look something like a bear or a walrus) and, more important than any of this, he had made a vow with himself that he'd never touch another drop of liquor as long as he lived.

11

"The greatest bloody bargain of my life."

The Larchmont Yacht Club in New York was a favorite of upper-class sailors. To it came naval officers and explorers as well as yachtsmen and amateur adventurers. In the early 1920s it was a place Bartlett often visited. He liked its big, dark dining room, built in imitation of a nineteenth-century ship salon, and he liked the people he met there.

One of his special friends was Commodore James B. Ford, an aging bearded patriarch who liked to wear a uniform jacket with braid and gold stars and to yarn about the sea. Ford was wealthy—one of the American superrich, with wealth that was both inherited and acquired. Among many other interests he was Vice-president of United States Rubber. One day in 1925, when he and Bartlett were dining together at the yacht club, Ford remarked that Bartlett looked like a lost soul.

"Why don't you buy a schooner and go sealing or fishing or something?" he asked.

"I couldn't raise enough money to buy a rowboat, let alone a schooner," Bartlett told him bluntly. At this point he was at absolute rock bottom, never expected to come up again.

Ford looked at him with a twinkle and a half smile.

"Go ahead and find your schooner," he said, "and when you've found her, let me know."

Coming from Ford, this was as good as a blank check. They finished their lunch and Bartlett went schooner shopping. He tried at first in Gloucester, Massachusetts, center of the American fishing industry, where some of the best schooners were usually to be found, but could see nothing that pleased him. He spent months looking for a ship that he could use, but nothing suitable seemed to be for sale.

Then he remembered a small schooner he had seen the year before in Brigus. She belonged to his cousin Harold Bartlett, who had recently purchased her. In spite of her age—thirty years—he'd been impressed with her lines and her reputation for strength and soundness. He wired and asked Harold to name his price. They haggled over it a bit, but eventually agreed on six thousand dollars. Then Bartlett went back to Ford, who simply wrote out a check for that amount and passed it over.

Bob now owned a schooner. Looking her over, he was convinced he'd got "the greatest bloody bargain of my life." What he might do with her was something else.

The *Effie M. Morrissey* was launched at Essex River, Massachusetts, on February 1, 1894. She was two-masted and clipper-bowed, ninety-seven feet long, with a ten-foot draft, and grossed a hundred and twenty tons. She had been built for fishing and named for the daughter of her first owner. Her builders were famous in their time, and she had certainly been one of their best ships. Her knees and stanchions and planking were all of oak; her deck was of white pine and her fastenings of Swedish wrought iron. Such a vessel was built to last. Properly maintained, she would never rot or wear out.

If you know ships, you can tell a great ship at a glance. A great ship, a thoroughbred, one that will perform perfectly in the most extreme conditions, has a look about her. There have been a few dozen such ships in the history of sail—many of them small; even back in the seventeenth century there may have been two or three of them: Peter Easton's *Happy Adventure*, Francis Drake's *Golden Hind*, Henry Mainwarring's *Princess*. In the nineteenth century there were the *Flying Cloud* and the *Marco Polo*. Among schooners there were only the *Bluenose* and a few others, among them the *Effie M. Morrissey*.

To achieve her true greatness, a ship must be wedded to just the right captain, with the combination of skill and boldness that can make full use of her best qualities. This clearly happened with the *Morrissey*. After three decades of an undistinguished career knocking about the fishing grounds, she finally found Bob Bartlett, a man worthy of her greatness; and during the next twenty years she proceeded to make twenty remarkable arctic voyages, accomplishing, almost incidentally, a vast enrichment of human knowledge, for Bartlett became an avid collector of scientific data and scientific specimens. He never asked to be paid for the work but was content with the loan of equipment and occasionally the loan of a scientist. Everywhere he went he operated plankton nets and otter trawls, took samples of water at all depths, and sent parties ashore to make collections of flora and fauna. The millions of specimens that he brought back from the Arctic, ranging from protozoa and mosses to the skeletons of whales, were all given free of cost to scientific institutions and entered as "gifts."

Up to this point Bartlett had been a daring navigator. He now became a careful amateur scientist, using his daring in a manner that put humanity permanently in his debt. The six-thousand-dollar gift that Commodore Ford gave him was the gift of salvation. In the *Morrissey* he not only forsook grandiloquence and found greatness, he also found the personal peace and fulfillment that he had been seeking down so many blind alleys during the first fifty years of his life. In his case the last twenty years were to be the best.

After Ford's gift, Bartlett went with new heart to former friends and backers, "scraping together every cent I could get" as either gift or loan. Then he bought the old Bartlett fishing rooms at East Turnivik, Labrador, which had been taken over by his father's creditors, and with them he acquired a wealth of gear and equipment. As a last resort, now, he could go fishing.

A trial run to Labrador in the *Morrissey* would be fine. One summer fishing, perhaps. Then, following the suggestion of a friend of his, the publisher George Putnam, he would begin a series of scientific explorations financed in part by taking with him the sons of wealthy men not as passengers but as paying apprentices. This kind of thing was popular at the time, the sons of the financial aristocracy getting a bellyful of adventure for a year or two before graduating from college and settling into the upper echelons of finance. What better grounding for any red-blooded American youth than to sail to the Arctic with Captain Bob?

So in the summer of 1925 he went fishing with the *Morrissey* on Labrador and encountered the same kind of luck he always had as a sealing skipper. It was a bad summer for ice. The *Morrissey* barely escaped being swamped by a foundering iceberg. As Bartlett described it, she escaped being sunk by approximately two seconds. But this wasn't, perhaps, as bad as it sounded. Narrow escapes were his specialty.

They were icebound and windbound and, at two different places, they missed making a great haul of fish by a mere two days. They kept working north (as schooners often had done before looking for the fish) until in late August they were in Saglec Bay, only a day's run from Hudson Strait.

Saglec, more of a fjord than a bay, is one of the most incredible places on the Atlantic seaboard. Though the fishing was poor, Bartlett enjoyed himself hugely. Moored between five-thousand-foot mountains under a colony of kittiwakes that numbered several thousand, he spent some of the happiest days of his life, puttering around the fjord in a small boat, playing amateur naturalist until the new ice making over the coves in late September warned him it was time to head for the open sea.

Back at Turnivik he found his men had taken a thousand quintals of cod (112,000 pounds). He loaded them on board the *Morrissey*, then took on more fish and passengers at Indian Harbour and headed for Brigus, running before a gale.

The *Morrissey* seemed to be in no danger. Running under reefed sails, with everything securely battened down, she was stanch and safe, even though water continually washed over her decks, and sometimes she shipped waves that struck her with a force of hundreds of tons. No gale of less than hurricane force could endanger this ship—or so it seemed.

But there was one member of the crew that Bob wouldn't trust on deck. He had taken his nephew, young Jim Dove, as cabin boy, after "overruling" his sister's protests. To make sure Jim didn't take risks on deck during the gale, he locked the lad in the after cabin. At the height of the storm there was a pounding on the companionway door and then an insistent hammering.

Going to investigate, he found the white-faced boy yelling that the ship was sinking. Hurrying below himself, he discovered that she was, indeed, or certainly would be in a very short time. One of the seas pounding down on the deck had smashed a cabin deadlight—a small heavy window designed to let in light from above and, if properly installed, just about failproof. No one on deck had noticed it, and the ship was filling with water. If the boy had not been below decks, the ship would have been past saving before anyone noticed that she was in trouble.

"Those ships that disappear without a trace," Bartlett noted, "encounter accidents like that one—freak things that no one can foresee."

In the gale, of course, they couldn't have launched a boat. Except, perhaps, for some deck wreckage, the *Morrissey* would have disappeared with all hands. Quickly, they made the deck tight and pumped her until the pumps sucked air.

Though the danger of losing her was averted, the ship continued to take a severe pounding all the way home, the strain on her being increased because she was fully loaded. When they took out the fish at Brigus, Bob expected to find a couple of feet of water in the bilges. Imagine his joy when he discovered that she hadn't leaked a spoonful— after thirty-one years of butting her way through the gales of the North Atlantic, she was still as tight as anything afloat.

Financially the voyage was a failure. Out of the full cargo that she carried, less than half was Bartlett's own fish. Worse, by the time they reached Brigus the season was so late that they missed the autumn market. The price of fish fell. Finally the merchant who agreed to take it was only able to pay half the contracted price in cash. The balance must remain on the books as a credit against outfitting for another season of fishing, the following year. Bob ended his first season as a shipowner deep in the red.

If he could help it, he decided, he'd do no more fishing. But at least he had made the acquaintance of a damn fine ship. He was convinced she could be converted to an exploring vessel, and he proceeded to refit her for work in the Arctic. First he would install a diesel engine while keeping the sails as her primary power. Then he would have her sheathed from keel to waterline with two-inch greenheart, one of the world's hardest woods from the forests of British Guiana, where Newfoundlanders sold some of their fish and bought most of their rum. Greenheart was the first choice of any experienced shipbuilder for use in ice. Bartlett also added to her equipment a pair of motor launches, carried on davits, to be used for inshore exploration.

The engine, he found, could be installed most economically in the States, but the sheathing was best done at Brigus. So early in the spring of 1926 he had her covered with the ironhard planking. Then he shipped a crew of Brigus men, mostly sailors who had served with him before, and they cleared port for New York, where he had arranged with a shipyard to install the engine.

This short run was one of Bartlett's worst passages. He ran into a long series of gales blowing from every quarter except the northerly ones that would have helped the ship on her way. She spent weeks at sea tacking against violent headwinds, was reported missing, and Bartlett arrived in time to read his own obituary notices in the American newspapers.

12

"God damn the keel! It's all or nothing now."

The first Bartlett arctic expedition, of 1926, was organized by George Putnam. He and his son David, thirteen, went along as working passengers. The expedition was mainly scientific, as Bartlett had wished. It was sponsored by the American Museum of Natural History and included a party under William H. Hobbs, from the University of Michigan. The *Morrissey* also carried four boatloads of supplies for Knud Rasmussen at the place he now called Thule.

Thirty-four people were jammed into the little ship, seven of them sleeping in hammocks in the saloon. The deck was a "sailor's nightmare with bundles of hay, canoes, tin boats, collapsible boats, rubber boats... Presumably everyone brought his own private transportation, whatever

suited his fancy. Fortunately, one of the two scientific parties was bound
for southern Greenland, not for Smith Sound and the Canadian Arctic
Islands.

By now Bartlett had his two motor launches. He also carried enough
diesel oil, in drums, for the whole summer.

They cleared from North Sydney, Nova Scotia, on June 26, and
headed north through the Gulf of St. Lawrence and the Straits of Belle
Isle. It was pleasant and easy going until they ran into the ice field off
Labrador on June 30. By now, however, they had a full twenty-four hours
of daylight every day. Even at midnight the northern sky was full of color,
staining the ice pans in unbelievable shades of green and magenta, and
they kept on deck all night long, watching the changing colors and the
flights of the first ice birds—ivory gulls, true arctic creatures, whose lives
are spent forever at the edge of the ice floes.

The little *Morrissey* proved ideal for this kind of navigation. With sails
stowed and the engine alone in use, she could zig-zag through the
narrowest leads of water, shouldering the ice aside as she went. After two
days of this, she got to the east and north of the ice, into open sea. The
sails went up again, in a brisk and favorable wind, as she went foaming
along toward Greenland, which the lookout sighted on July 5. It was a
place called Sukkertoppen, an island just south of the Arctic Circle in
Davis Strait. In spite of the ice they had made an excellent passage,
covering the 1,440 miles from North Sydney in nine days.

They landed the party from the University of Michigan the next day,
then headed for Disko, the only large island on the east side of Baffin Bay,
with the settlement of Godhavn—the place where Bartlett had picked
up the southernmost stragglers from the Crocker Land Expedition in
1917.

It turned out to be one of those years when the ice was lighter than
usual, and the *Morrissey* everywhere made good passages. She crossed
Melville Bay in twenty-nine hours, compared with the twelve days it had
taken Bartlett to make the same passage in the *Neptune*.

Near Thule (where they were to land Rasmussen's supplies) they
anchored cheek by jowl with an iceberg, and here one of the Americans,
new to the north and to the ways of ice, almost sank them. He got out

his rifle and began taking pot shots at the ice cliff towering above them.

"The minute I saw what was happening," Bartlett recalled, "I hollered for full speed on the engines and ordered them to slip the anchor chain. There wasn't a second to lose. Those big bergs are often precariously balanced, and even the report of a gunshot may make them start to founder."

This one, indeed, began to roll. Bartlett himself was at the wheel and saw the ice coming down over his head.

"If we'd tried to get the anchor, it would have been the end of us," he said. They let the chain run out, while the engine raced, and the captain looked astern to see if the falling ice was going to clear the main boom, which projected far over the counter. It cleared, he estimated, by "about a boat-length."

Next day they landed Rasmussen's supplies. Then they ran on north of Thule for a place called Inglefield Gulf, in Kane Basin. They were now in the most northerly part of the navigable Arctic, beyond all human habitation.

Here, at full high tide and going full speed ahead, Bartlett ran the *Morrissey* hard aground on a ledge of rock. Fortunately, no sea was running. But as the tide fell she began to roll over farther and farther until she was lying right on her side, her masts parallel with the water. They laid out kedge anchors to try to hold her and shifted all the cargo they could shift, in the six hours between full high and full low tide. Then all they could do was wait and see if she was going to roll over and sink.

"A toss-up, I'll tell you," Bartlett admitted. "There was deep water just a couple of fathoms to port. If she rolled over into it, that'd be the end of her."

The falling tide was slack for a while, then, imperceptibly at first, began to flow. They breathed again. She wasn't out of trouble, by any means, but her death had at least been postponed.

While the tide rose, they worked like galley slaves to lighten her, hoping that she might float a little higher and that they could winch her off the few feet that would be needed to clear the ledge. The tide inched higher and higher, and the bosun kept measuring it and reporting to the captain.

They took all the strain the winches could exert on the kedge anchors. She didn't move an inch.

"It's stopped rising," the bosun reported. "It's a foot lower than it was last time, skipper."

It began to fall, with the Morrissey as hard aground as ever.

While the tide fell once more, and rose once more, they continued to empty her of cargo. At the top of the next high tide they still couldn't move her. It began to fall for the third time. She had now been aground for twenty-five hours. As the ebb went on, a storm started to come up from the westward, and that looked like the end of it. A sea running over the reef would soon pound the little ship into driftwood.

By now they had taken everything movable out of the ship and run it ashore in the launches. When she went down, at least they'd be well provisioned. They could go by launch to Etah and get help. They were not in personal danger except perhaps for the men who were trying to make her float.

With the storm still coming up, but no great sea running, the tide reached the full for the third time and began to turn. The ship still wouldn't move and was now, by all the laws of reason, doomed for an absolute certainty. But in this last emergency, Bartlett demonstrated the resources of desperation. He ordered the crew to hoist the mainsail.

"You can't!" the bosun gasped. "You'll rip the keel out of her!"

"God damn the keel!" Bartlett roared back. "It's all or nothing now. Lively on those bloody halyards, God blast your souls!" The mainsail went up in seconds.

And just then, the Bartlett luck returned. As the halyards were made fast and before they'd even touched the sheet, they caught a back squall of wind from the highland on the starboard beam, "hitting the mainsail with a smack you could hear." The ship rolled over to port until her rail went under. Then she began grinding and bumping and pounding over the rock, and then, suddenly, she was in deep water and floating upright. A marvelous combination of luck and daring and split-second judgment had saved her from what seemed to be certain destruction.

You could see her settling in the water as she ran around a point into a little harbor. Here they anchored and began the backbreaking task of trying to keep ahead of the water that was pouring in through the holes in her bottom; men who had already worked without sleep for thirty-eight hours now had to man hand pumps. At this point a whole band of Inuit from Etah showed up and volunteered to man the pumps.

Bartlett found that by continuous pumping the ship could be kept afloat, so he ran her south six hundred miles to Upernavik, to the south of Melville Bay, the northernmost Greenland port where help might be obtained, and here he beached her to make repairs. Then another miracle happened. Knud Rasmussen arrived in a motor launch with a professional diver, and two of those pressurized space suits that divers used to wear. Finding this kind of equipment more than five hundred miles north of the Arctic Circle in the 1920s was truly a chance in a million.

Rasmussen, who could do anything climbed into the second diving suit, and the two of them got down under her bottom. There they not only repaired the leaks but sawed off the false keel that had been twisted athwartships. The main keel was practically undamaged. In a matter of hours the *Morrissey* was seaworthy again. Then off they all went, with Rasmussen and his friend on board, and anchored in Thule harbor, where they celebrated with a party that went on all one night and lasted halfway through the next day.

That was the end of the summer's mishaps, and Bartlett got down to serious work with his plankton net and otter trawl and sounding equipment. They made collections in Smith Sound and in Jones Sound, between Ellesmere and Devon Islands, and later in Lancaster Sound and in Pond Inlet, running westward to Eclipse Sound, south of Bylot Island.

In spite of the early troubles, they accomplished an excellent summer's work, which promptly established Bartlett's reputation with the American scientific institutions. From that time forward he had no trouble getting the backing of such groups as the Carnegie Institution and the American Museum of Natural History, but in those days, budgets were so tight that he always had to look for additional financing from one place or another.

On their way back to Greenland from the Canadian Arctic Islands, they ran across a swimming polar bear, a female accompanied by two cubs. They shot the bear and lassoed the two cubs, taking them back to the New York Zoological Society.

At Holsteinborg, in the great ice-free area of western Greenland that lies to the north of the Sukkertoppen ice field, they picked up Professor Hobbs and his party. They, too, had enjoyed a most successful summer in the field and had made a large collection of specimens and data.

The southward trip was slower than the northward one. In the Labrador Sea, just south of Davis Strait, they lost their propeller. This, however, was not a major disaster. At that time of year they would not have to navigate in ice, and the new suit of sails with which Bartlett had fitted the Morrissey could drive her at eight or nine knots in a favorable wind.

They arrived at L'Anse an Loup, Labrador, nine days after leaving Holsteinborg, for an average run of a hundred twenty miles a day. They docked at Sydney, Nova Scotia, on September 22, for inspection of the bottom and temporary repairs. There they found that their propeller had been improperly installed in the first place. Its loss was due to electrolytic action, the effect of two incompatible metals immersed in salt water, and not to the grounding or to ice damage.

Though the Morrissey had barely survived her first voyage into the High Arctic, inspection on dock showed that she had suffered surprisingly little damage. The greenheart sheathing had saved her from being stove and sunk, and except for some recalking, she was ready to face the ice once more. Needing no major repairs, she was laid up for the winter.

The passengers, amateur and professional, had gotten more than their money's worth. Two of them, Dan Streeter and David Putnam, published books about the voyage. (David Goes to Greenland was a real Boy's Own thriller. The opportunity was almost too good to miss. How many thirteen-year-olds have been shipwrecked in the Arctic?)

Bob Bartlett, too, began writing, about this and previous voyages. Within a year, assisted by the same man who had ghost-written Robert Peary's books, he had completed his The Log of Bob Bartlett and Putnam had agreed to publish it.

13

"...as ominous as derelicts..."

Putnam's first voyage with Bartlett pleased him so much that he offered to arrange another for the following year, this time into one of the most legendary sections of the Arctic—to Foxe Basin and to Fury and Hecla Strait, the narrow, ice-choked channel that opens from Hudson Bay to the northwest.

Almost from the time of the Cabots, men had been trying to go westward by this route without success.

Hudson, Frobisher, Bylot, Baffin, to name only the most famous, had come to grief among these desperate ice fields three and four centuries before. From Foxe Basin, Jens Munk, with sixty-four men and two ships had turned southward, back in 1619, seeking a westward passage out of Hudson Bay for the king of Denmark, had been caught by the winter and frozen in, and had watched his men drop dead one by one until only three, besides himself, remained alive. An expedition of fifty men seeking a route into Foxe Basin for the Hudson's Bay Company in 1719 had perished to the last man, no trace of them being found until forty-eight years later.

William Edward Parry, one of the great English explorers, and the man who came closest to getting through the Northwest Passage in a sailing ship, had finally reached Fury and Hecla Strait in 1821, demonstrating at last that there really was a passage westward out of Hudson Bay, though one by which no ship could sail. It was named for his two vessels, the Fury and Hecla. (He lost the Fury later in Lancaster Sound, which he correctly guessed was the true northwest passage.)

Fury and Hecla Strait is not only narrow and ice-choked, hut has an ice stream flowing eastward through it. Bartlett at first considered tackling this impassable channel by the only way that it might possibly be done from the north by way of Lancaster Sound and the Gulf of Beothic. Since the flow is eastward from the Gulf of Beothic into Foxe Basin, it might be possible, in some years, to enter the arctic pack in the gulf and allow a ship to he carried by the ice through Fury and Hecla Strait into the waters opening into Hudson Bay. He was deterred from this quixotic scheme by the practical Putman. They were going north for the Museum of the American Indian and the Heye Foundation to gather scientific data, not to be the first ship to circumnavigate Baffinland, attractive as that scheme might look to a romantic like Bartlett.

They sailed from Brigus on June 23, 1927, bound first for Sculpin Island, Labrador. They wished to explore it because legend insisted (and still insists) that there was once a Norse settlement on this barren rock, surrounded, as it is, by the ice of the Labrador Current. The archaeologists on the Morrissey did find evidence that the island had once been wooded, though nothing resembling a tree had grown there In recent centuries. They also found the ruins of old Inuit stone-and-sod houses, similar to the one Cook had found on Melville Island, nineteen years before, but nothing that looked like the remains of European settlement.

Rounding Cape Chidley, the northern tip of Labrador, on July 4, they were caught between large ice floes. Their shaft was broken, and their propeller was carried away. They were several days trapped in the ice before they could get clear and beach the ship to repair the shaft. Then they made a good run to Amadjuak on the west coast of Baffin Island, where the Hudson's Bay Company had established a tiny post. At Amadjuak they took on an Inuit pilot, who guided them to Cape Dorset. From there they ran into Foxe Channel, where they shot one polar bear and lassoed another. While they were hoisting the captured one on deck, it got loose and "treed" all hands in the rigging except the Mate, Will Bartlett, who had enough presence of mind to dive down the companionway, grab a rifle, and put a bullet into the bear before it could wreck the ship's topsides.

Somewhere near Cape Dorset, they ran aground in thick fog at half tide. Tidal range in that region is enormous, only a little less than the highest in the world. Spring tides may easily top forty feet. By the time the ebb was finished (the tide was falling when they went aground) the *Morrissey* rested on bare rock, and you could walk around her without getting your feet wet.

They laid out anchors to hold her against what they knew was coming. And then, when it did come, she was almost wrecked. A six-foot tidal bore swept down on her: a solid wall of black water capped with hissing spray. They measured the tidal flow and found it was running at a speed of seven knots. The five-inch manila anchor line was snapped like a piece of thread, but the other anchor, attached to a heavy chain, held fast. The bottom of the ship took a severe pounding, but she stayed where she was and within a few minutes was afloat, with several feet of water under her keel.

Then, tearing past on the seven-knot flood tide, the ice arrived— pans and floes and even small icebergs—growlers, as Newfoundlanders call them. If one struck the *Morrissey* at seven knots, she'd either be stove in or carried with it over the ledges and reefs as wreckage. The fog was still thick.

"I stood at the wheel peering forward, and not a damn thing could I see beyond the foremast," Bartlett wrote. "The lookout on the bow would sing out that a big floe was standing in, and to go over to port, *quick*. I'd spin the wheel hard over and the *Morrissey* would sail herself as far to port as the anchor line would permit. The water stream on the rudder from the tide was the same as though we were under way, and the schooner handled beautifully. We had to risk breaking out the anchor. It was another case of taking a long chance in preference to waiting for sure destruction.

"I was at the wheel for several hours, listening for the hails from the lookout on the bow. I couldn't see him. He'd yell to swing to starboard, or to port, and I'd do it. Staring out into the murk I'd see a low, dull mass of tumbled ice sweep by us, only a few feet away. Stray growlers bounced off the hull, shaking us badly. The water was as black as ink. And under that fog the ice didn't look white. It was a dirty gray, and as ominous as the derelicts it resembled."

At the top of the flood, the lead line showed thirty-six feet of water over the top of the rock that had been dry at the ebb. Considering what had happened, they got off with amazingly little damage—a few cracked planks—but their rudder, propeller, and keel were all still in place, and the ship still fully seaworthy.

Bartlett next headed north to the supposed location of the Spicer Islands, finding nothing there except empty sea. Despite his report to the American Geographical Society, these islands were still shown erroneously on American maps for the next twenty years.

He guessed that the islands so mapped were really parts of the mainland of Baffin Island, whose west coast, north of the Arctic Circle, was at that time totally unknown. Eventually, the Spicer Islands disappeared, but new islands were found, considerably to the east of their reported position, some of them so big that they had, indeed, been thought to be part of the Baffin Island mainland.

Bartlett got north on that trip as far as Fury and Hecla Strait, which he found was solidly plugged with ice. He then ran back to Cape Dorset, picked up the parties of scientists that he had left on Baffin Island and headed home. It had been a successful reconnaissance of one of the least-known parts of the world.

Six years later he made a much more careful survey of the same area, doing a detailed cruise along the west side of Foxe Basin. On the later voyage he visited Coral Harbour and Repulse Bay, went through Frozen

Strait, westward around Southampton Island, and coasted the whole length of the Melville Peninsula.

He landed a party at Barrow River and photographed the great waterfall where Parry's men, after a bitter winter in the ice, found flower-decked valleys and took off their boots to run through the grass, pretending they were home in an English meadow.

Just north of here he found nests of white gyrfalcons, rough-legged hawks, and peregrines. Because there were no accurate charts, or even proper maps, of Foxe Basin, they kept a masthead lookout and often sent a motor launch prowling ahead to smell out the shoals. They anchored at the island of Igloolik, at the entrance to Fury and Hecla Strait, and the archaeologist Junius Bird here recovered a clay pipe, the only relic he could find of the Fury and Hecla expedition that had wintered on the island more than a hundred years before.

This time they succeeded in getting into Fury and Hecla Strait, where they found numerous walrus and bearded seals sleeping on the ice pans, but they were unable to force a way through. They then returned to Igloolik and excavated its abandoned Inuit village for the Museum of the American Indian.

Here, in 1933, in the least-visited corner of the Canadian north, where no one had ever sunk a spade before, they made their most valuable collection of Inuit relics. Here, too, Bartlett found Inuit who were still hunting without firearms, men who had never used a gun, living entirely off land and sea with the aid of their traditional weapons, using none of the white man's goods, but with plenty to eat and wear. They were, he reported, the healthiest and most prosperous people he had seen anywhere on his arctic voyages.

The *Morrissey* had an ice-free passage southward through Hudson Strait into the Labrador Sea. It was an almost trouble-free voyage until they reached Domino Run going south along Labrador. Here, with a heavy following sea, she bounced off the bottom three times in quick succession, and, looking astern, Bartlett could see the water breaking white right from the bottom. He described it as his "closest call," though considering the other hairbreadth escapes that were almost routine for the *Morrissey*, there might be two opinions about that. His nephew Jack

Angel, who sailed with him as photographer and engineer, said this incident convinced him of the vessel's indestructibility. After banging rock bottom three times, she didn't leak a spoonful, and in fact they didn't even bother to put her on dock until she had to go on for her refit the following year.

The two voyages to Fury and Hecla Strait not only supplied new information about the natural history of the region and its archaeology, but about its geography also. In fact, as George Putnam pointed out, they completely redrew the map of Foxe Basin. It was the first time the area had been visited by geographers except under extreme duress, while looking for the Northwest Passage. Bartlett's two expeditions were like holiday cruises. He made numerous soundings, new to the charts, and took time to make extensive collections with his plankton net and trawl.

Bartlett's collections of marine fauna provided the material for a work on the fishes of Greenland, Labrador, and Hudson Bay, which was published by Yale University in 1937.

No further scientific exploration was made in that part of the Arctic until the time of the Second World War.

14

"...like a human being in torment..."

After a voyage to the western Arctic to collect skeletons and grave goods in 1928, and a motion picture cruise to Labrador in 1929, Bartlett resumed his work in the eastern Arctic, this time in one of the least-known parts of the earth, northeast Greenland.

If you glance at a map of the north, you might assume that eastern Greenland is easy to approach, while its west coast, hemmed in by islands and ice-choked channels, is difficult. The reverse happens to be true. Baffin Bay is relatively free of ice in summer; an experienced pilot with a properly equipped ship can usually get as far north as Etah, which lies within 12° of the pole. East Greenland is quite a different proposition. The major outlet from the Arctic Ocean is the great strait, three hundred miles wide, between Greenland and Spitzbergen. Here the ice flows southward, unimpeded, from the North Pole itself and indeed from the whole arctic basin, forming the world's worst ice field all the way along the western edge of the Norwegian Sea and the Denmark Strait, reaching Cape Farewell at Greenland's southern tip, and turning north-ward into Davis Strait.

Some years it is possible to get inside this two-thousand-mile ice field and to cruise northward along the coast through open lanes of water. Other years it is impossible to reach the east coast of Greenland at all, except perhaps with a modern icebreaker. The West Ice, as it is called, is so heavy that it prevented the Norse from ever colonizing this coast, and at times made it difficult even for the Inuit who followed them.

The first East Greenland Expedition was undertaken, in 1930, for the Museum of the American Indian, one of its objects being to locate and excavate the ruins of Inuit villages. Bartlett, with his incurable taste for phrases out of dime novels, referred to it as "the land of the Lost Eskimos." They were "lost" only in the sense that they had abandoned east Greenland villages because the hunting was lean, and there was better hunting elsewhere. Inuit had always done this, wherever they lived.

After visiting Iceland, the Morrissey ran north for six hundred and thirty miles to the latitude of Shannon Island, keeping in open water to the east of the ice field all the way. Then from July 9 to 11, she worked her way westward through the ice until she reached coastal water and got within nine miles of the land. Here she tied up to an ice floe and sent a party ashore by komatik.

This, and the land to the north, was the home of the "Lost Eskimos," people reported by whaling ships of the eighteenth and early nineteenth centuries to have lived there "in thousands." Junius Bird and Hans Brun were left on Shannon Island with a tent and supplies to make an archaeological dig, while the Morrissey made a collection of specimens in coastal waters. Working conditions were perfect, the weather was clear, and since they were six hundred miles north of the Arctic Circle, they had twenty-four-hour daylight.

Then an easterly gale came up, the ice moved in, and the Morrissey got solidly jammed among pans that piled up into rafters far higher than her deck. The ship was lifted out of the water by rafting ice and jammed between sheets as the Karluk had been jammed sixteen years before. She "groaned like a human being in torment," Bartlett said. He ordered all supplies on deck, ready to move to the ice, then gave the order that every captain dreads to contemplate. "Stand by to abandon ship."

The motor launch was swung out, to be landed on the ice and salvaged for later use, and every man on board got ready to jump for his life. But her bottom didn't cave in. The oak ribs and oak planking and greenheart sheathing strained and buckled and held until the pressure slowly began to ease, and they were carried along the line of the ridge like something being squeezed out of a tube. Then a crack appeared ahead. It widened into a lead. And suddenly they were free. Such are the caprices of an ice field under pressure.

They then worked their way north to Germania Harbour (approximately another hundred miles), made some photographs, located more Inuit ruins, and went bear hunting, without success, around Cape Bismarck. From here Bartlett turned south again, fearful of leaving the two archaeologists and their helpers—a party of four altogether—stranded on Shannon Island. So he missed his chance to visit the great glacier fronts of King Frederik VIII Land, as he might easily have done that year, because there was open water far to the north. The chance was never to be repeated. On all his subsequent voyages to east Greenland, the ice made it impossible to get north of Germania Land. He made his farthest north on that coast nine years later, just a few miles beyond his record of 1930.

He found there, only seven hundred fifty miles from the pole, "an ice-free land knee-deep in grass, with flowers blooming and herds of musk ox grazing." Thousands of barnacle geese and pink-footed geese were nesting among the golden poppies and the purple saxifrage. To the naturalists, this was an arctic paradise, the sort of place that gives birth to the legends of semitropical valleys in the polar regions. From it, they brought home thousands of specimens, representing hundreds of species, for the Smithsonian Institution and the New York Zoological Society.

To Bartlett it seemed one of the most beautiful coasts on earth, with cliffs up to five thousand feet high, glaciers, ravines, and cascades. Bird colonies were everywhere, and there were huge icebergs on all sides. He was so delighted that he mixed his metaphors with wild abandon: "We wormed our way in and out through a galaxy of white and blue cathedral spires."

In Denmark Strait, midway between Iceland and Greenland, in clear sunshine, he and his mate, Will Bartlett, saw one of the most remarkable mirages ever reported. At 63°42´N., 33°42´W., they had a clear view of the mountains of Iceland, including the unmistakable peak of Snaefells Jokull, a headland northwest of Reykjavik that rises to 4,744 feet.

Bob Bartlett was standing at the wheel of the *Morrissey* at the time, and calling Will to his side, he asked him to estimate the distance of this conspicuous coastline. Will, a thoroughly experienced sailor, took a look at it and replied, "Twenty-five to thirty nautical miles."

As a matter of fact, the land they were looking at was between 335 and 350 statute miles distant. This remarkable happening, even though it occurred only once in the lifetime of the twentieth-century's greatest ice captain, goes a long way toward explaining the Norse voyages of the ninth and tenth centuries. If it happened once to Bartlett, then it doubtless happened once or twice to Eric the Red and Leif the Lucky and the other explorers of that time. There would be rare occasions when they could plainly see the mountains of Greenland from the northwest coast of Iceland and the mountains of Baffinland from the east side of Davis Strait. Such mirages probably revealed most of the new lands they discovered, and the courses they would have to sail to reach them. So these remarkable seamen were lured westward until they discovered and explored a large chunk of North America almost five centuries before Columbus.

Altogether, Bartlett made four expeditions to northeast Greenland, adding immensely to the scientific knowledge of this little-visited part of the world. His work there was sponsored by eight major scientific organizations. In addition, on all of his voyages he collected oceanic and atmospheric data for the American Navy.

His troubles were frequent, and his escapes were many and various, but he had a miraculous knack for getting out of the most deadly jams without serious harm. During the *Morrissey* voyages—some of the most daring expeditions ever undertaken in a schooner—he never lost a man. He never regarded his men as expendable. The sailors were all personal friends from Brigus, some of them brothers and nephews (he had an immensely strong sense of family), and the scientists were mostly personal friends too, men like Junius Bird who went on sailing with him year after year.

It would not be right to suggest that life on the *Morrissey* was all hardship. Bartlett preserved a dinner menu among his papers, dated July 4, 1931, when he was eight days north of Iceland and not far from Germania Land. Besides roast veal with sweet potatoes, peas, and beets, they had such trimmings as tomato juice, queen olives, Florida preserves, orange ices, chocolate layer cake, nuts, figs, and candy, topped off with a Petit Gruyère St. Bernard, a good French champagne, and a flask of cherry brandy.

But these were no mere holiday cruises. They added more to human knowledge and to the opening of the north than all the heroics of men like Peary and Cook. Because Bartlett was engaged in real work rather than in the kind of publicity stunt that the newspapers and the National Geographic Society so dearly loved, he received small recognition for it. But the recognition that he did receive came from the highest sources. On January 19, 1931, the American Geographical Society, received the following cable:

WITH CONGRATULATION ROBERT BARTLETT'S SPLENDID BRILLIANTLY ACCOMPLISHED EXPEDITION EAST GREENLAND, SEIZE OPPORTUNITY BEHALF DANISH POLAR EXPLORERS SEND CENTURY'S GREATEST, BOLDEST, MOST EXPERIENCED ARCTIC SKIPPER OUR GREETINGS AND ENTHUSIASTIC HOMAGE.

KNUD RASMUSSEN

It was the last great days of the arctic game animals, and they did a fair amount of hunting both for meat and for museums. Bartlett brought home the first narwhal groups that had ever been seen in North America, making plaster casts of the animals, as well as securing skeletons. He provided dozens of musk ox, walrus, and polar bears for zoos, as well as heads and skins for museum collections.

Bartlett's observations of arctic birds and mammals, made over more than half a century, gave him cause to worry. He not only saw the extinction of the Eskimo curlew (it had been one of the most popular game birds in his childhood) but the widespread decimation of the eider duck colonies. Their flocks, numbering hundreds of thousands, were reduced in his lifetime by hunting and egg gathering and the commercial collection of down from their nests until many of the islands where they nested were entirely deserted. As early as 1926 he noted that "egging" the arctic islands no longer provided the easy supply of food that it did in 1898.

During his later voyages, he reported that the big-game animals were much scarcer than they had been during his voyages with Peary, a fact also remarked by MacMillan, who went through one whole summer north of the Arctic Circle without seeing a single bear. They do not seem to have understood that their own hunting had depleted the animals, though if Bartlett had stopped to reflect that a polar bear needs a territory of dozens or even hundreds of square miles, he might have guessed that killing scores of them in a single season could make a big difference to their numbers.

The nearest he came to such an admission was to comment on the increasing scarcity of walrus right through the 1930s. Even then he wondered if narwhal might not be driving them away. Driving them where? It was the sort of suggestion made time and again by hunters. The game wasn't being exterminated by guns. It was being "driven away" by some other animal—a common rationalization in the days before field biology had delimited territories and habitats.

There can be no doubt, in fact, that the parties of American hunters, taken north by Peary and Bartlett and MacMillan to help finance their expeditions, continued effectively the work of destruction begun by Peary when he organized wholesale slaughters of Canadian big-game animals to feed the armies that he sent marching toward the pole and, in the end, did a good deal to reduce walrus and bears and musk ox from relative abundance to their present state of scarcity.

15

"...so close, you could easily throw a biscuit ashore...."

On a beautiful Saturday afternoon, August 24, 1935, Bartlett left Brigus in the *Effie* M. *Morrissey* and sailed into a hurricane.

He'd been told bad weather was on the way, but he had been sailing through storms for half a century and he ignored the warning. His mother had been listening to the radio—there were, by that time, two stations in St. Johns—and hearing weather forecasts that predicted winds of seventy miles an hour. All ships were advised to seek shelter. She begged Bob to stay over Sunday.

Besides, she urged, "you could go to church with me."

That was all Bob needed to hear. His taste for church, and all other aspects of religion, had been thoroughly knocked out of him in childhood. From time to time he sent money to the United Church minister at Brigus, but not for the church. It was earmarked for his private use and was, in fact, used to build a greenhouse attached to the manse. He shook his head.

"Promised to get those youngsters home before the first of September," he said. "The weather looks civil enough, and nothing can hurt the *Morrissey* anyway."

He was convinced his little ship was unsinkable, and so were the regular members of the crew. His mate, Will Bartlett, and his engineer Jack Angel, both said they had the feeling that nothing could send her to the bottom. She certainly was one of the strongest ships of her class ever built.

Besides, tropical storms that come prowling north along the American seaboard from the Caribbean have a habit of missing Newfoundland. Their usual course is northward until they reach the edge of the Grand Banks, where they tend to curve eastward, well to the south of the island, and spread themselves into a vast area of gales in mid-Atlantic. Only about once in ten years does a hurricane predicted to hit Newfoundland actually do so.

As was now his custom, Bob had a shipload of millionaires' sons, not as passengers, exactly, but as "apprentices." They had spent the summer with him in the Arctic, doing their full share of the work in fair weather and foul, and now they were heading home to their academies and boarding schools and military colleges to continue the process of being converted into he-men.

The *Morrissey* stood out across Conception Bay with her sails drawing nicely. But as the sun set, there were ugly-looking clouds gathering.

"Looks greasy, sir," said Jim Dooling, the bosun. "And this morning there was a winddog."

Bob had been seeing winddogs, or sundogs as they were also called, all his life. They occur usually after dawn or before sunset, small "suns" on one or both sides of the real sun, sometimes connected by a halo of light. They are caused by a kind of cloud that occurs only rarely—a thin, highly dispersed stratum of ice crystals at enormous altitude. This cloud is usually at the extreme leading edge of a major storm center.

Bob went below to look at the barometer.

"Bottom has dropped out of it," he said when he came back on deck. "We're going to get some wind all right."

Still he kept on. Nothing could happen to the *Morrissey*.

At 10 P.M. they rounded Cape St. Francis and set a course that would take them five miles east of Cape Spear, a headland just south of St. John's, the most easterly point in North America. They were now only two hours' run from the city, with its perfectly safe harbor, where they could take shelter if need be.

Just as they rounded the cape and turned toward the southeast, they ran into a long, heavy swell, running up from the south. The wind was still light, but the swell could only be caused by a big storm. It might, however, be two or three hundred miles away.

The radio operator was obviously worried. He kept bringing storm warnings to Captain Bob.

"At last I told him to forget it and turn in," Bartlett recalled. "You didn't need a radio by now to know that there was a storm somewhere off to the south."

A little before midnight they could see the lights of St. John's, six or seven miles on the starboard beam, and hear the dismal groaning of the horn on Cape Spear. Bartlett had now made up his mind. He was going on. St. John's was the last harbor they could safely enter north of Cape Race. A ship attempting to run into Ferryland in a storm is taking a last desperate chance. Better to stand off to sea, if possible.

The watch was changed at midnight and a new group of apprentices came on deck. Then there was a rustle of wind and a sudden gust of rain. It was "as dark as the grave and about as reassuring," Bartlett said afterward. Storm petrels came on board and went waddling about the deck, and the boys discovered that you could pick them up in your hands—they were far tamer than barnyard fowl. These small black-and-white birds, known to Newfoundlanders as "mother Carey's chickens," spend their lives on the wing, far from land, except in the nesting season, and seek the shelter of a deck only in a gale or when lost in a dense fog. They cannot take off from a flat surface, and must jump from a height, such as the edge of a cliff, to become airborne.

Suddenly, looking ahead, Bartlett could see a wall of total blackness sweeping down on him. Then the ship was hit by a deluge of falling rain and sudden savage blasts of wind.

He ordered the engine stopped and hauled the ship under sail farther to the eastward, seeking to keep as much sea room as possible between himself and the land. Fortunately, he had not set the mainsail, and the ship now ran off under foresail and jibs. The wind quickly increased to a whole gale, and then to something more than a whole gale.

First the lee rail went down into the water, and then the whaleboat covers went under, as well. Bartlett knew that there would be a lull in the wind before it reached its greatest velocity, and he was waiting for it. In the lull he hoped to be able to lower the foresail and take a double reef in it. Then, with reefed foresail and jibs, he'd be ready to ride out the hurricane. He never got the chance to try this plan. During the first violence of the storm, before the wind dropped even temporarily, the foresail let go with a noise like a thunderclap, blown right out of its bolt ropes. Shreds of canvas snapped wildly from gaff and boom.

The ship was now on a lee shore, almost without sails, and the engine alone would never be able to keep her from being blown on the rocks. The immediate problem was to get past Bay Bulls Head and the Witless Bay Islands, but the whole coast from Cape Spear to Cape Ballard runs almost north and south, a stretch of more than fifty miles where any gale from an easterly point is deadly dangerous to a sailing ship. Fortunately, they had gotten to the south of Cape Spear before the hurricane hit, and thus had a couple of extra miles of sea room-perhaps seven miles in all.

Everyone on the ship worked desperately to get out a new foresail, and bend it, ready-reefed, to boom and gaff. The wind now reached eighty to eighty-five miles an hour, and the storm trysail went the same way as the foresail.

The ship was being blown relentlessly ashore, and the only hope of saving her was to get the new sails rigged. But they had to work on deck, or just above deck, in a wind of hurricane force, with rain water and sea water mixed in a common deluge and waves sweeping the ship. In such conditions, even men working for their lives were slow, and it took three hours of pure nightmare to get the new sails set.

---

* Newfoundlanders have always given their bearings in compass points, which, in that province, are approximately 30°, counterclockwise, from true bearings. North-east, in

In the hour before dawn the wind dropped slightly, but the waves rose even higher than before and the ship rolled more heavily, a sure sign that they were getting into shallow water, near land. There was too much noise to hear the surf, if there was any, but they waited moment by moment for the fatal crash, while Bartlett coaxed a single extra point of southing out of the ship in the hope of clearing whatever lay ahead. If they drove ashore in such a wind, there wasn't a chance in a thousand that any of them could survive.

As the blackness turned gray with dawn, they could see an ominous line of white in the darkness ahead.

Breakers.

As the light increased a little more, there was the black loom of a cliff, with sheets of white spray flying hundreds of feet into the air along its face.

Bartlett tried for another half point to windward and ordered the reefs to be shaken out of the foresail. To try to squeeze past that headland, he would have to risk being dismasted. She lay over in the water, with her boom just missing the wave tops, heading out to sea but making so much leeway that they couldn't be sure if she would clear the cliff or not.

Were there rocks off the headland? They didn't know. They hoped not, but everyone was unconsciously braced for the crash that they expected from moment to moment.

There were no rocks. They were skirting a perpendicular cliff face that dropped right into deep water. They were so close, "you could easily throw a biscuit ashore." Then, suddenly, they were in the open, around the cape, with the land trending off in a southwesterly direction. They breathed again and got back on a southerly course.

As the day brightened, the wind dropped down to a whole gale, then to half a gale, and slowly veered around. Out on the Banks they passed a schooner—a banker—with her mainmast gone, but not in need of help, still able to sail under jury rig. Later they learned that she had lost three men overboard, that another ship had been lost with all hands, and that altogether thirty-four men had been drowned on the east coast of Newfoundland that night.

But Bartlett's incredible luck (helped out, this time, by superb

---

Newfoundland, is close to true north. However, because the compass is meaningless in the High Arctic, all bearings in this book are reckoned from astronomical north.

seamanship) had held once again. Except for the loss of a couple of sails, the *Effie M. Morrissey* had come through the hurricane with no damage whatever. No one on board had been hurt.

Bartlett saw to it that he was reported safe by the wireless station at Cape Race, which relayed the news to St. John's and thence to Brigus, where his family was gathered around a battery-powered radio set (the power lines had been blown down by the storm) waiting for news.

Then he sailed into New York in triumph and landed his crew of apprentices after the sort of experience that hardly one man in a thousand lives to tell about.

16

Wheaties, Winchesters, and Walrus.

Throughout the 1930s Bartlett continued his annual voyages into the northern ice—four to Germania Land and other parts of eastern Greenland, six to northwest Greenland, Ellesmere Island, and other parts of the Canadian Arctic.

Except for the privately financed voyage of 1932, to erect a memorial to Peary at Cape York, north of Melville Bay in Greenland, his voyages were all collecting expeditions for museums and scientific societies.

He loved the work so much that he turned down the opportunity to take Richard Byrd to the Antarctic. Bartlett and Byrd were old friends, and when Byrd had trouble finding a ship, Bartlett suggested the *Bear*, the ancient barkentine that had rescued the Greely expedition half a century before and had attempted to rescue the *Karluk* survivors. She was lying at a California dock at the time, waiting to be broken up for scrap, and Byrd got her for $1,050. But Bartlett refused to sail in her.

Byrd wanted him so badly—or perhaps the prestige of having the century's greatest ice navigator on his expedition—that he got in touch with Dr. Wilfred Grenfell, the man who had founded the famous medical mission in Labrador, and asked him to persuade Bartlett to reconsider his refusal.

Grenfell's letter of persuasion is a classic. He thought it important that a "Britisher" should share the glory of the South Pole with Byrd. He urged Bartlett that going captain of the Byrd Expedition to "Little America," as they called it, would be the greatest service be could render to "The Empire," and indeed to humanity.

Bartlett obviously knew better. Any competent captain would be good enough to land the American expedition on the Antarctic Continent, and since Byrd was going to the pole by aircraft, he wouldn't need the sort of hard-driving sledge master that Bartlett had become. (Byrd used dogs only locally, but they were important. Among his supplies for the expedition were 100,000 pounds of dog food and six cases of chewing gum.) Bartlett, on the other hand, now had half a century of arctic experience, and he was making the best possible use of it every year. He had reached the time of life when years should not be wasted.

Continuing to finance his own voyages through the Depression was by no means easy. He used a number of devices to keep himself afloat in the thirties. For one thing, he continued to lecture to any society or group that could afford to pay him, accepting fees as small as twenty-five dollars a night, and on rare occasions getting as much as a hundred and fifty.

He signed "endorsements" for various products. Winchester firearms were the only ones good enough for an arctic explorer. Wheaties for breakfast made you fit to face a polar bear. Pullman cars were a better way to travel than dog teams.

Sometimes the advertisers, perhaps in financial trouble themselves, welched on their payments. There is a letter among his papers complaining to the Pullman owners that he hadn't received a cent for endorsing their sleeping cars the year before, and asking for a round-trip ticket,

New York to Chicago so he could accept a lecture engagement and earn himself a badly needed hundred dollars. He got his ticket, but apparently that was all.

By now Bartlett had a fair eye for photography, both film and stills. His nephew Jack Angel was documenting each voyage with spectacular photographs, and they made numerous reels of silent film. It was a time when every movie house, in addition to its features, padded out its programs with cartoons and short subjects, one of the regular shorts being a "news" package. This created a hungry market for odds and ends of film ranging in length from about half a minute up to two minutes or occasionally longer. A polar bear charging a hunter, a walrus struggling in a sling as it was hoisted on board a ship battering its way through the ice, or an archaeologist uncovering a skeleton, all made good copy. Pathé News, one of the wealthy film companies of the era, put Bartlett on staff as a roving editor at a salary of $3,900 a year. He had no fixed duties. They merely supplied him with film, and they had first pick from whatever footage he brought back from his voyages.

He wrote for the Sunday supplements, published articles in the *National Geographic*, and, following the success of his Log, wrote *Sails Over Ice*, which came out in 1934 and failed to earn him enough royalties to meet his tobacco bill.

At that time he was still smoking a pipe. Lit or not, it was always in his mouth, lying beside his plate, or on a bedside table. Jack Angel, worried that he would fall asleep with the pipe in his mouth and perhaps set fire to the ship, made a smoking stand with a pipe holder for the Skipper's cabin.

"That was the end of his smoking," Angel recalled. "He quit while we were fitting out for the next voyage." After forty years of total addiction to tobacco, he tossed the pipe over the side and never touched the drug again.

The men didn't like it, and Bartlett overheard them growling about it: "The old man is hard enough to get along with at the best of times," Bosun Jim Dooling complained to a shipmate. "Now that he's quit smoking it's going to be plain, unadulterated hell."

In the end Bartlett gave away most of the copies of his last book, many of them to friends in Newfoundland who could never afford to buy a copy in those lean and hungry times. Almost everyone was on his uppers (often literally) and even in New York few people were buying such luxuries as books. But throughout the thirties Bartlett continued to find a few young men whose families owned entrenched wealth and were willing to pay a thousand dollars each to have them taken to the Arctic with Captain Bob as working passengers.

Some of them sailed year after year and grew to feel very deeply attached to the captain. One letter, surviving among his papers, is from a youngster who had made several voyages with him and was now being forced by his family to seek wider experiences. He wrote to assure Bartlett that he would rather be with him on the Morrissey than anywhere else in the world and that his absence this year would be by necessity and not by choice.

The brothers and nephews who sailed with him—Jim Dove, Robert Dove, Jack Angel, Sam Bartlett, Will Bartlett, and Rupert Bartlett—went as crewmen, some on a fixed salary, some not. But even to those who went without any promise of pay, he was extremely generous throughout those lean years, and Angel says, "It was largely on money he gave me that I went through McGill University." Two of his volunteer crewmen became doctors, one an engineer, one a lawyer, later a judge. He sent money home to his mother every time he wrote—which was often—and he supplied the farm at Brigus with thoroughbred livestock from American breeders.

Besides fees from Pathé News and from working passengers and small contributions from scientific institutions (often only a few hundred dollars each: they, too, were feeling the pinch), the sale of live animals that he brought home for zoos helped to finance the Morrissey expeditions. Here is an account by Jack Angel of the capture of a young walrus near Cape Sabine, Ellesmere Island:

"Just at midnight on July 30, 1935, the schooner Effie M. Morrissey, under the command of Captain Bob Bartlett, was making her way along the edge of the great paleocrystic ice floes that extended as far as the eye could see up into the Kane Basin, completely blocking any further progress to the north. We had reached a point where the Canadian and

Greenland shores were equidistant from us and only a few miles away. The Canadian shore was covered with snow and glaciers, cold and unwelcome. The Greenland shore which we had followed on our way north looked warm and inviting, its towering hills covered with talus at the base of which there seemed to be a little vegetation. In between the hills the glaciers wended their way back to the great Greenland ice cap, the largest iceberg factory in the world. We had reached our 'farthest north' for that year, and for a few hours were lying quiet, drinking in the peacefulness and sinister beauty of our surroundings.

"As we skirted the heavy ice, we came upon a herd of walrus on an ice pan. Walrus often come up on the ice, and if the sun is very warm they get sunburned. When found in this condition they actually have to be driven into the water. Then you will hear them cry and snort with pain. On this occasion, however, while the sun was high it lacked the heat of noonday, and at our approach the walrus slipped off the ice and into the water, disappearing among the loose pans. One little fellow however became separated from the rest, and the captain was persuaded to lower the whaleboat and to go after it, for I suggested that we would be able to get some pictures of it on the morrow and could then let it go.

"So with thrilled hearts we lowered the whaleboat and went after the baby walrus. For perhaps half an hour we followed it in and out among the ice pans, for we could see it as it swam under water. Every time it came to the surface we would try to grab it, and finally managed to get a boat-hook around one of its flippers. With eager hands we grasped its fore and hind flippers and hauled it into the boat.

"The way the baby walrus wriggled and barked made us laugh so heartily that we almost lost him several times. We managed to get a spinning rope around his body, as one would harness a small dog, and on reaching the side of the *Morrissey* hoisted him, none too gently, to the deck. Once aboard, the baby was given the freedom of the ship, but to our dismay he was able to get his plump little body over the gunwale and had to be hauled back time after time. He barked continuously, and I almost went on my hands and knees to him to make him stop, because the captain was none too pleased about the noise. Several days before, we had built a large crate for narwhal skeletons which we were bringing back to the Field Museum of Natural History in Chicago. In exasperation we put the walrus in the crate and tied the skeletons to the rigging."

"To us on the *Morrissey* the baby walrus became known as 'Pee-uk,' an anglicization of the Eskimo word for 'good.' After association with the Eskimos for several weeks, everything, whether good, bad, or indifferent, was termed 'Pee-uk.' So why not the baby walrus?"

Rupert Bartlett also described a walrus hunt, this one mainly for meat, with the incident capture of three young walrus, on the voyage of 1940:

"Fortune favored the 1940 trip, for on arriving at Robertson Bay we found Jim Van Hauen of the Copenhagen Museum of Natural History. Jim was staying there for a short time with the Eskimo folk and wanted to obtain a supply of walrus meat for his dogs and Eskimos. So the captain offered to help him with the *Morrissey*. Jim accepted the offer and agreed to help us capture four walrus pups alive. In a few hours we steamed out of Robertson Bay with Jim and two of the best Eskimo hunters aboard.

"The party later transferred to a whaleboat and the Eskimos got into kayaks. A few miles through the ice brought us to an open lake of water with hunks of ice in it. Herds of walrus could be seen rising to the surface to blow. It was agreed that the Eskimos would stalk the walrus and harpoon them when they got within range. Men in the whaleboat would then shoot the animals.

"Several herds seemed to appear from nowhere. The nearest one contained at least thirty-five animals. A large cow walrus was spotted with a young walrus pup riding on her back. No matter how violently the mother rolled and plunged, the young one clung to her with its pliant pair of little flippers."

The walrus spotted the hunters, and sounded their warning calls, something like "awik! awik! awik!" The hunters then drove their kayaks into the midst of the herd, and the slaughter began. One of the men harpooned a walrus, then leaped out to an ice pan and wildly waved for the whaleboat.

"We were surrounded by a forest of gleaming ivory tusks," Mr. Bartlett recalled. "Some of the brutes attempted to climb over the side of the boat. Others favored the even simpler method of making entrance through the bottom. Happily, we withstood all attempts at invasion, and indeed, with the help of a couple of rifles and boat hooks, succeeded in driving most of the herd off.

"Jim Dooling, one of the party, had armed himself with an Eskimo harpoon with which he was very skillful, and watching his chance he succeeded in harpooning a cow with a young pup on its back. The rest of the herd by this time had dived to the bottom leaving us with the harpooned cow and the pup, who was far from captured yet. A young pup will only stay with its mother so long as she is alive, so we dared not run the risk of shooting her until we had secured the little chap."

Using a lasso, they tried time and again to rope the pup as its mother came up for air, eventually succeeded, then shot the mother and tied the carcass to the boat.

"We had been so engrossed with our own work that we had forgotten our Eskimo hunters, but now we heard excited shouts, and, looking around, saw the two of them standing on a pan of ice, with two walrus pups securely tied up and ready for shipment to New York."

On that voyage of 1940, Bob Bartlett got farther north than he had on any voyage since leaving the *Roosevelt* in 1909. It was the year the *Morrissey* established her own "farthest north" of 80°33´ in Kennedy Channel on the northeast shore of Ellesmere Island. It was a fitting way to celebrate his sixty-fifth birthday.

Next year he took a government expedition to northwest Greenland for scientific work. The United States was not yet involved in the war that had been going on in Europe, but France had fallen to the German Blitzkrieg, it looked as though England might fall any minute, and there was speculation about an attack on North America, one possible route being by way of Iceland and Greenland. Hence the appropriation of government money for "scientific" expeditions that were really military in nature.

Besides the *Morrissey* in northwest Greenland, they sent the *Bear*, the *Northland*, and the *North Star* to northeast Greenland. Though not at war with Germany, they nevertheless captured a German ship, loaded with radio and weather equipment, and towed it to Boston—an invocation of the Monroe Doctrine, Greenland being regarded as in the American sphere of influence, that constituted the first act of war between Germany and the United States in the Second World War.

Then Bartlett began to consider retirement. He had built up the farm at Brigus. His mother was still living there, old and frail but mentally vigorous, as her numerous letters to her famous son attest, and he was still deeply attached to her—the only woman, apparently, who was ever important in his life. There is a long-standing tradition of master mariners retiring to farms, and Bartlett certainly meant, eventually, to join the thousands of his peers who had already done so. He might have chosen to do it as early as 1941 had not the American Government commandeered his ship for war work.

Japan attacked the United States on December 7, 1941, bringing America reluctantly into a war that had been raging for more than two years in Europe and Africa and for more than five years in China. The American Government had already decided that an air-supply route would be needed by way of the Canadian Arctic and Greenland to northern Europe. Bartlett and the *Morrissey* were obvious choices for a share of this work.

They made out an order commandeering the schooner as a supply ship for use in Hudson Bay and Greenland. Bartlett was, of course, far too old to be conscripted for war duty, but he volunteered to go with the ship, and his whole crew from Brigus volunteered to go with him: Will Bartlett, his brother and mate; Len Gushue and his son Bart, engineers; William Pritchard and his son Tom, cooks; George Bartlett, Charles Batten, James Dooling, able seamen; James Hearn, radio operator.

They would be doing, as part of the war effort, what they had been doing all their lives—navigating through the ice fields, taking supplies to arctic bases, pioneering, with echo sounder and lead line the way for the bigger ships that would eventually abolish the whole life of the north as they knew it.

17

"The war that wasn't worth fighting."

Bartlett's war years were spent on some of the most arduous voyages of his life. Unlike his private expeditions that began in June and ended early in September, they ran from April until well into October and sometimes into November.

His logs of those years say surprisingly little about the war or the kind of work he was doing—survey and supply. He filled his pages, instead, with the information that had always interested him most, with bulletins from the immortal side of life, with news of buntings and little auks, with accounts of snow stained red and green by living creatures too numerous to imagine, with the incredible colors of arctic sunrise, and with the magic of poppies blooming along the ice foot of a glacier.

And he collected poetry, as he had been doing most of his life. When a piece of writing, prose or verse, in a magazine or a newspaper pleased him, he clipped it and pasted it in his log, then wrote around it in such cramped longhand that his entries become illegible. Though he had spent many of his middle years urging governments to use twentieth-century technology to investigate the mysteries of the sea and of the arctic basin, he was, in the 1940s, both by taste and by inclination, still a nineteenth-century man.

He also went back to reading the classics. He discovered a particular love for Wordsworth, reading and rereading such long narratives as *The Prelude* and *The Excursion* and commenting on their qualities.

He seems not to have cared much about the war, and his few remarks about it were derogatory:

"I wonder if winning...is worth fighting for?"

He also privately detested the people he worked for. The career militarists in charge of the war effort struck him as stupid, wasteful, inept, and uncivilized. They filled him with dismay and made him doubt that victory could be anything but an empty sham. Why fight for such barbarians against the barbarians on the other side?

His handwriting had now become shaky at times—especially early in the mornings—and he collected obituaries of his famous friends. But these secret symptoms of age were confined to his logbooks. On deck he still looked like a walrus on an ice floe, and he could still produce a bellow that might be heard five miles away if the wind was in his favor.

He continued to enjoy life to the full, not only in his beloved Arctic but also ashore in New York during the winters, where be divided his time between the Murray Hotel, his official residence, and his ship, with frequent visits to Broadway and Fifth Avenue.

He was now on top of the world once more, his years as a "mangy lion" not only surmounted but so thoroughly forgotten that most people never suspected he had lived through such a period at all. He was now the Grand Old Man of the North, going to parties, dinners, receptions, and, between these social activities, to all kinds of entertainments—to the opera, to musical comedies, to burlesque shows, to Carnegie Hall to hear a performance by Rachmaninoff. His winter logs had such notations as:

"Saw Noel Coward's marvellous movie" and "Went to the Plaza for Explorers' banquet."

His nephew Jack Angel says he was lonely. That, perhaps, was inevitable in an aging, single man, living thirteen hundred miles from his family. Angel saw him often in New York—a short train ride from Montreal, where Angel was taking his engineering degree. They went to public entertainments together, including some of which Angel's mother would scarcely have approved. But lonely or not, he led a full life twelve months a year.

Every moment he could spare from other activities, he buried himself in a book. He read and reread the accounts of all the great arctic explorations until he could quote them from memory almost verbatim. But he read everything else, too—the novels of Jane Austin and the Brontë sisters, for example. (He pronounced them "marvellous.") His room in New York was filled with a jumble of books and arctic souvenirs, heads and skins and narwhal tusks and Inuit handicrafts. His bunk on the *Morrissey* was piled so high with books and magazines that he slept, always, on the floor.

Even though he had published three books, two of which had been financial failures, he cherished the ambition to publish others. He wrote and rewrote and typed up hundreds of pages of notes dealing with his childhood and youth, with his experiences as a sailor, with the opinions and theories he had developed over more than half a century at sea and among the ice floes. If these had been collected, completed, and edited, as he intended, they would have produced his best book—mature, reflective, honest, Walden-like in its rambling, but full of insights and unexpected pleasures for the reader.

He also began a biography of Sir Wilfred Grenfell, the English doctor who had spent most of his life in northern Newfoundland with summer trips to Labrador, and had founded a public service organization that amounted to a private empire. Bartlett pursued the Grenfell biography at considerable length, but laid it aside and never finished it.

Some of his manuscripts and many of his other papers were lost or destroyed. Some survive only in fragments. Among his papers there are some intriguing curiosities, including complete ships' logs, in his handwriting, dealing with voyages made not by him but by other members of his family. He must have copied these logs from originals. But why? Perhaps he also cherished the ambition, sooner or later, to work on a family history—hardly surprising, since a history of the Bartletts of Brigus would have included the entire story of the Newfoundland seal hunt and most of the important voyages of arctic exploration between the 1850s and the 1940s.

In 1942 Bartlett was sent to Hudson Strait and Ungava Bay to help establish the two bases that were then known by the code names of Crystal One and Crystal Two. Later, they were to become military, and then civilian, airfields at Chimo (Quebec) and Frobisher Bay, altering forever the pattern of Inuit life in Canada's eastern Arctic.

The Chimo field was thirty-five miles upriver from the sea—a river that had never been sounded, and rarely, if ever, navigated by anything bigger than a small supply boat operated by the Hudson's Bay Company. Bartlett took the *Morrissey* up the Koksoak River, "scraping bottom all the way," as he wrote in the *National Geographic*. The trip was especially hair-raising because the tide at the river mouth rises and falls a full forty feet. When he got to the embryo air base, where freight planes were already landing on a dirt strip, and met the hydrographic crew who were to survey the river with him and do a detailed chart of the approaches in Ungava Bay, one of them cracked: "We don't need to take soundings now. Captain Bob already knows how deep the water is. He bounced all the way in."

They spent twelve days in the Koksoak, sounding and marking a channel for cargo ships, and laying out work for the dredges that would follow them. Then they sailed for Baffin Island.

Frobisher Bay, at that time, had never been charted and only occasionally visited. It was still an Inuit preserve, wild and beautiful. Though never surveyed, it had been mapped by the remarkable nineteenth-century explorer Charles Francis Hall, who had gone north entirely on his own, without money and without backing, and spent several years living with the Inuit as one of them, totally adapted to their way of life and completely in love with it. (Incidentally, Hall was one of the first white men to extend them the courtesy of calling them Inuit rather than Eskimo.)

His map of Baffinland had shown Frobisher Bay for the first time as a bay rather than as a strait between islands. After Hall's sketchy investigations, it was another eighty-two years before Bartlett arrived with an echo sounder backed up by a lead line to chart its bottom. In the bay he found a curious hazard that he had never encountered elsewhere—numerous pinnacles of rock so incredibly steep, and rising from such depths, that some of the surveyors thought they were picking up echoes from whales rather than from the bottom. These rock spires rose from depths of five hundred feet almost to the surface, like the towers of great underwater cathedrals. Between them, he charted a channel through which the American armed forces freighted into Frobisher so much prestressed concrete and structural steel that they created in this icy wilderness what amounted to a city, filled with chewing gum and jukeboxes and pinball machines, on the site where Hall had slept in an igloo, dined on frozen seal meat, and "enjoyed it exceedingly."

At Frobisher, the tide was an even greater problem than at Chimo. It had a range of forty-five feet, with a tidal bore as savage as anything ever seen in the Bay of Fundy. But the channel was marked and, where necessary, dredged and blasted, the docks were built, and Frobisher became one of the principal links in the chain of bases extending around the rim of the Arctic between North America and Europe.

Next year Bartlett sailed again to Hudson Strait on supply work. But in 1944 and 1945 he was back among his old friends the Greenlanders, east and west. The war, he discovered, had sent the Inuit of Smith Sound back to the ways of their ancestors. It was good for something, after all. They had given up wearing clothes made from trade goods. They had stopped eating bread and drinking tea and coffee and had returned to a diet of meat. Their clothing was made of sealskins and musk-ox furs. The change, in his opinion, was very much for the better. Already they seemed healthier and happier than he had ever known them to be while working for the white men in exchange for things like candy and flour and tobacco and tea.

During the half-century that Bartlett had known them, the Smith Sound people had gradually forgotten their primitive hunting techniques and had come to rely completely on firearms. Then the war not only stopped the flow of trade goods but cut off the supply of ammunition as well. They were thrown back on their own resources—whatever they could recover of them. A few old-timers (among Inuit, anyone who reaches the age of fifty is an "old-timer") taught the young men how to hunt with the harpoon and how to stalk game at close quarters. Bartlett was surprised at the success with which these almost-forgotten skills were recovered and became convinced that if ever the white men abandoned the Arctic, the Inuit would bounce right back to become its lords and masters, just as they had been before the white invasion began.

The Americans in Greenland had made no effort to adapt to it and, in general, thoroughly detested the country. Those at the lonely weather stations on Greenland's east coast were "Wild with delight" when the *Morrissey* arrived to take them off after a year of total isolation. Such bases still could not be supplied by air. Runways were too expensive and took too long to build, and helicopters were still a thing of the future. The best the government could do was to change personnel annually during the two or three months in summer when a ship could reach the coast.

Bartlett spent his seventieth birthday eating bear meat in Melville Bay. To celebrate, he threw a party on board his ship, inviting a number of Greenland Danes who had been marooned in the High Arctic throughout the war because their home country had been overrun by the Germans. They didn't know, he said, that they were eating bear. Seeing the big red roasts come out of the freezer, they assumed it was "a delicacy packed in the United States" and ate it with great enthusiasm.

That was the day Japan surrendered and the war came to an end. And it was almost the end of Captain Bob Bartlett's voyaging.

On the way south, he visited the ancient settlement of Godthaab and the even older one of Julianehab, to which Eric the Red went as an exile to found in that uninhabited land a republic that survived for four and a half centuries, but was doomed in the end by one of the periodic advances of the everlasting ice, and perhaps also by the advance of the Inuit, then entering Greenland for the first time from the west. The Norse had never learned to meet this land on its own terms, but had endeavored, to the end, to convert it into farm country.

On this last voyage, the *Morrissey* came closest to losing one of her crewmen. Almost miraculously, she had survived twenty annual trips into the ice fields of the eastern and western Arctic without once suffering the fatality that was forever threatening.

Now, in her home waters, crossing the Bay of Fundy in November, she ran into one more gale. But she was snug and seaworthy and in expert hands. Bob Bartlett was so sure of her, and of his crew, that he was down in his cabin, curled up with a book, while the storm blew its worst.

Suddenly he was roused from his reading by a tremendous crash overhead. The *Morrissey* had shipped one of those giant seas that occur when one big wave overtakes another and their height and bulk are combined. Bartlett rushed on deck. His brother Will was gone, swept over the side.

"As I went over," Will recalled, thirty years after it happened, "I heard the voice of our dead bosun, as plain as I've ever heard anything in my life, saying, 'You're gonna be all right, Will.' And you know, it's a strange thing, I wasn't frightened. There was a coil of rope washed out with me, right alongside, and I caught it and hung on, and then I was washed back toward the ship by another sea, and I could hear Bob hollerin' from the deck, and he could hear me hollerin' from the water."

So Bob hauled Will back on board, not only safe but completely unhurt, and he returned to Brigus and his family, while Bob spent one more winter in New York.

18

"His ship goes sailing on...."

A Newfoundland seaman isn't necessarily old at seventy, and though the war was over and the *Morrissey* released from government duty, Bob Bartlett still hadn't made up his mind about retirement. In New York he returned to his winter routine of reading, writing, and going to parties. He rose every morning at six and ate at a restaurant near his hotel. It was before their usual opening hour, but he had made a deal with them to bring in one cook and serve him breakfast.

He completed another article for the *National Geographic* magazine. He wrote up his log faithfully, noting wind and weather and the day's activities just as though he were still at sea. But he was unsure about the future. The *Morrissey* lay in dock, awaiting refit, while her owner postponed making plans for the summer.

April came, and he caught a "spring cold," the sort of thing he had endured every year of his life while growing up, when his mother had used "tons of linseed meal" in chest poultices. This time it refused to go away, but he refused to take it seriously.

"He would have died in his hotel room," his brother Will said, "if it hadn't been for a visit from Jim Dove."

Jim, one of Bob's nephews, was a doctor, and he was shocked to find the Skipper, as they all called him, lumbering about the streets of New York with what he instantly recognized as a case of pneumonia. Dove rushed him off to a hospital.

By the standards of the time, Bartlett got the very best care and treatment. But at the end of the Second World War, pneumonia was still one of the major killers, yet to be attacked successfully by antibiotics. Physical strength seemed no defense against it. Bartlett, indeed, seemed strong and even cheerful, joking and flirting with the nurses, as he had always done with women. Nevertheless, three days after admission he died. It was April 28, 1946.

The American papers published glowing obituaries, often neglecting to mention that he had been born in Newfoundland and had made most of his voyages in ships of Canadian registry. In Canada, except in St. John's, Newfoundland, where he was still regarded as a national hero, his death was largely ignored.

"When I heard he was dead," Jack Angel said, "I couldn't believe it at first. He had seemed to all of us as indestructible as a rock. I just couldn't visualize the Skipper coming home in a box.

"I went up to New York—it still wasn't easy, in those days, to get there in a hurry from Newfoundland; it was still surface travel all the way, but I got there in time to see him in the funeral parlor. I was the only person from Newfoundland present that evening, or at the funeral service the next day. After the service I went with the body by train and boat to Port aux Basques, where I met Captain Will, and passed the body over to him to be taken home to Brigus for burial." (Angel himself lived at St. John's.)

So Captain Bob rejoined his shipmates in the earth where both his parents, and so many other Bartletts, were buried. The grave was marked by a simple stone in the churchyard. Those men who ventured to the ends of the earth and dared the worst of its seas often had the knack of surviving its hardships and returning, in the end, to the village where they had been born.

The Bartletts are still in Brigus. "Hawthorne Cottage," which was Bob Bartlett's home during his brief visits to his native town, is still in the family. It has been owned successively by his surviving sisters and by his nephew, Judge Rupert Bartlett. The farm where he and Will and his cousin George played as boys is also still in the family, a flourishing farm with cattle and chickens and sometimes with ducks and geese, now in the fifth generation of family ownership.

His ship not only survived him but began a third career almost as long and successful as her two former ones. After Bartlett's death, the unsinkable *Effie M. Morrissey* continued to sail the oceans for the next thirty years and, even yet, may not have made her last voyage.

She survived a fire in harbor and then lay abandoned, apparently left to rot, but was salvaged and refitted as a yacht for use in the tropics. She never did service in this capacity, however, but instead was sold, in 1949, to the Portuguese, who by then had become the owners of most of the world's ancient ships. She then went into service as a transatlantic packet, running between American ports and the Cape Verde Islands.

Her Portuguese owners eventually retired her to the interisland trade, in which she continued in service, until the spring of 1976.

During the 1960s the Government of Newfoundland announced plans to purchase her and moor her in one of the outport harbors as a maritime museum and tourist attraction. But having made this announcement, they did nothing about it. The few thousand dollars needed to bring the *Morrissey* home were never voted by the legislature.

In 1976 the *Morrissey* was purchased by "friends", including former Cape Verde Islanders living in the United States, and left to cross the Atlantic once more for the Sail Past at the United States Bicentennial celebrations in New York. After that she was to be laid up in the United States maritime museum at Mystic Seaport. She ran into a storm of hurricane force and was dismasted in mid-ocean. She had to be towed back for repairs. At last report she was still in the Cape Verde Islands, and an American committee was trying to raise the additional funds to pay the repair bill so that she could be brought to the United States, where it was proposed that she might be used as a school ship before being retired to Mystic as a permanent memorial to her former master and to the age of sail in which he lived.

Appendix A

Annotated List of Bartlett's Voyages

Only northern voyages and sealing expeditions are included. He made others, in southern latitudes, as a merchant seaman, merchant captain, and naval commander.

1892. In *Panther*, with father. A successful sealing voyage.

1893. Temporary skipper of schooner *Osprey* on Labrador voyage.

1894. In *Panther*, sealing in Gulf of St. Lawrence. The Bartletts brought in a full load of hood seals, one of the few times it was ever done. Unlike the harp, the hood is a comparatively rare species.

1894. Full season as Skipper of the *Osprey* on Labrador voyage.

1895. In *Panther*, sealing in Gulf of St. Lawrence. They missed the young seals entirely, but made a "saving trip" by securing half a load of adult seals at the end of the season.

1896. In *Iceland* as First Mate (known as "Second Hand" on sealing ships) for a very successful voyage. Again they missed the young seals, but secured 10,000 beaters (seals that have taken to the water) and 2,000 old harps and bedlamers (subadults).

1897. First Mate on a bumper sealing voyage. They began killing on March 14, loaded the ship in seven days, leaving 4,000 pelts on the ice (another ship got them). They arrived at Harbour Grace March 23, for a round-trip of nineteen days, one of the fastest ever to the Gulf ice field. Then they made a second trip.

1898. First Mate in *Hope*, sealing in the Gulf. Landed 16,000 pelts.

1898. First Mate on the *Windward* to Ellesmere Island with Peary.

1900. First Mate of *Hope*, landed full load of whitecoats, including 5,ooo pelts carried on deck.

1901. First command of a sealing ship, the *Kite*, a small barkentine, 190 tons net, with a crew of 107 men. A most unusual voyage. After loading 7,000 whitecoats they drove out of the Gulf of St Lawrence in an ice jam, got free, and followed the seals back into the Gulf, farther and farther until they reached the mouth of the Miramachi River in northern New Brunswick. Right alongside the Miramachi breakwater they shot 1, 200 adult seals, but recovered only 300. The others sank. They grounded near Escuminac Point but were carried off the shoal by drifting ice. At Richibucto Bay they hit bottom "fortunately not hard," Bartlett noted in his log. They got back to St. John's after all these adventures with only half a load. It was a bad year for the Bartletts. William, Robert's father, lost the *Hope* in an ice jam that spring.

1902. First Mate of the *Algerine* at the seal hunt.

1902. First Mate of the *Algerine* with his uncle John Bartlett as Captain, to Cape Wolstenholme, Hudson Bay.

1903. Captain of the *Nimrod* at the seal hunt. A failure.

1904. Captain of the *Nimrod* at the seal hunt. On this voyage he poached 4,000 seals on a Sunday. He was in danger of drawing a blank. He almost did anyway. Those 4,000 illegal seals were the only ones they got.

1905. Captain of the *Algerine*, his most important appointment as a sealing skipper up to that time. The voyage was a failure.

1905. Captain of the *Roosevelt* with Peary in the Arctic.

1907. Captain of the *Leopard*. Shipwrecked, total loss.

1908. Captain of the *Roosevelt* with Peary in the Arctic.

1910. Captain of the *Beothic* on voyage to Greenland and the Canadian Arctic Islands.

1912. Captain of the *Neptune* on sealing voyage.

1913. Captain of the *Neptune* on sealing voyage.

1913. Captain of the *Karluk*, Canadian Arctic Expedition.

1915. Captain of the *Bonaventure*, one of the new ice-breaking ships built especially for seal hunting. He got a quick load for his most successful sealing voyage. His total catch of seals, in eight voyages as master, was 80,093, a poor record, considering that four of these voyages were made in sealers of the larger class. His father, who commanded small ships, had landed 444,801 pelts, averaging 11,000 to a voyage.

1917. Captain of the *Neptune*, to the rescue of the Crocker Land Expedition.

1925. First voyage as Captain of the *Effie M. Morrisey*, Labrador. All the following voyages are on the *Morrissey*.

1926. Northwest Greenland. American Museum of Natural History and University of Michigan.

1927. Western Baffin Island and Foxe Basin. American Geographical Society, Museum of the American Indian, Heye Foundation.

1928. Siberian Arctic. American Museum of Natural History.

1929. Labrador. Photographic expedition sponsored by Maurice Kellerman.

1930. Northeast Greenland. Museum of the American Indian.

1931. Northeast Greenland. Smithsonian Institution, Heye Foundation, American Museum of Natural History, New York Botanical Gardens.

1932. Northwest Greenland. Sponsored by Peary family and supporters, to erect Peary monument at Cape York.

1933. Foxe Basin and Fury and Hecla Strait. Museum of the American Indian, American Museum of Natural History, American Geographical Society.

1934. Ellesmere Island and northwest Greenland. Philadelphia Academy of Natural Sciences.

1935. Ellesmere Island and northwest Greenland. The Field Museum, the Smithsonian Institution.

1936. Ellesmere Island and northwest Greenland. The Field Museum, the Smithsonian Institution, the American Geographical Society, the Chicago Zoological Society.

1937. Ellesmere Island and northwest Greenland. The Smithsonian

Institution, the Chicago Zoological Society.

1938. Ellesmere Island and northwest Greenland. United States National Museum, the Cleveland Museum of Natural History, the Smithsonian Institution.

1939. Northeast Greenland. New York Zoological Society, the Smithsonian Institution.

1940. Ellesmere Island and northwest Greenland. The Smithsonian Institution, Vassar College, U. S. Navy Department.

1941. Northwest Greenland. Survey work for the American Government for entry of that country into World War II.

1942. Ungava Bay and Frobisher Bay. Survey work for Allied bases, Crystal One and Crystal Two.

1943. Frobisher Bay. Supply and survey work for military bases.

1944. Southern and eastern Greenland. Supply and service of weather bases.

1945. Northwest Greenland. Supply and service for military bases.

Appendix B

List of medals, with citations, awarded to Captain Robert A. Bartlett

1. The Peary Polar Medal, awarded by Congress of the United States for the 1908-09 expedition.
2. Medal of the American Geographical Society, awarded for geographical research, 1925.
   Medal of the Royal Geographic Society, awarded for arctic exploration 1886-1909. The medal was designed by the wife of Robert Falcon Scott and presented at Albert Hall before an audience of 10,000 by the society's president, the son of Charles Darwin.
   Medal of the Explorers' Club, presented to "The leading ice navigator of modern times."
   Medal of the Geographical Society of Philadelphia, "For the discovery of the North Pole."
3. Medal of the Italian Geographical Society for reaching 87°48′ N. It was presented in person by the king of Italy.
   The Hubbard Medal of the National Geographic Society, "For attaining the Farthest North, 87°48′, March 31, 1909."*
4. Medal of the Harvard Travellers Club, "For Arctic Exploration 1914."
5. "The Back Grant," awarded by the Royal Geographical Society, in recognition of leadership in the Karluk disaster of 1914.

---

*The Hubbard Medal is perhaps the world's most exclusive honor. In seventy years it was awarded only ten times for such feats as the discovery of the poles, the conquest of Everest, and the first solo flight across the Atlantic.

Appendix C

Bibliography

This is a list of the more important Bartlett sources from which this book was created and certain other, related works that were consulted extensively. It does not include newspaper interviews or magazine articles by, or about, Bartlett.

Apleton, T. E. *Usque ad Mare, a History of the Canadian Coast Guard.* Ottawa: Department of Transport, 1969.

Bilch, Edwin Swift. *The North Pole and Bradley Land.* Philadelphia: Campion and Company, 1913.

Bartlett, Harold. *History of Brigus.* St. John's, Nfld.: The Newfoundland Historical Society, 1940.

Bartlett, Robert A. *Northward Ho! The Last Voyage of the Karluk.* Boston: Small, Maynard and Company, 1916.

———— *The Log of Bob Barlett.* New York: Putnam, 1928.

———— *Sails Over Ice.* New York: Scribners, 1934.

———— "From the Crow's Nest" (MS). Newfoundland Archives, St. John's.

———— Miscellaneous papers (MSS). Newfoundland Archives, St. John's.

Chafe, Ernest F. "The Voyage of the Karluk and Its Tragic Ending" (MS). Newfoundland Archives, St. John's.

Condon, Michael F. *The Fisheries and Resources of Newfoundland.* St. John's, Nfld.: The Newfoundland Historical Society, 1925.

Cook, Dr. Frederick A. *My Attainment of the Pole.* New York and London: Mitchell Kennerley, 1913.

———— *Return from the Pole.* London: Burke Publishing Co. Ltd., 1953.

Diubaldo, Richard J. "The Canadian Career of Vilhjalmur Stefansson" (MS). London, Ont.: University of Western Ontario, 1972. Microfilm in National Archives, Ottawa.

Henson, Matthew A. *A Negro Explorer at the North Pole.* New York: Arno Press, 1969.

Horwood, Andrew. "Captain Bob Bartlett in the Arctic," St. John's, Nfld.: CBC tapes, interviews, and comment with Ernest Chafe and Rupert W. Bartlett, 1970.

Koryakin, V. S. *Was Frederick Cook at the North Pole?* Moscow: Academy of Sciences of the U.S.S.R., 1975. Translation by W. E. Ricker, 1975.

Mamen, Bjarne. "Diary of Canadian Arctic Expedition, 1913-1914" (MS). National Archives, Ottawa.

McKinlay, William Laird. *Karluk.* London: Weldenfeld and Nicolson, 1976.

Mowat, F. *The Polar Passion.* Toronto: McClelland and Stewart, 1976.

Peary, Robert E. *The North Pole.* London: Hodder and Stoughton, 1910.

Putnam, George Palmer. *Mariner of the North.* New York: Duell, Sloan and Pearce, 1947.

Rawlins, Dennis. *Peary at the North Pole; Fact or Fiction?* Washington, D.C.: R. B. Luce, 1973.

Stefansson, Vilhjalrmur. *My Life with the Eskimo.* New York: Macmillan, 1919.

———— *The Friendly Arctic.* New York: Macmillan, 1921.

Index